The Pickleball Effect

SCOTT MANTHORNE

Copyright © 2025 by Scott Manthorne
All rights reserved.

No part of this book may be reproduced, stored in a retrieval system, or transmitted in any form or by any means—electronic, mechanical, photocopying, recording, or otherwise—without the prior written permission of the publisher, except for brief quotations used in reviews or critical articles.

Published by Atlas Elite Publishing Partners
Formatting by Michael Beas

eBook ISBN: 978-1-962825-71-9
Paperback ISBN: 978-1-962825-72-6
Hardback ISBN: 978-1-962825-73-3

This is a work of nonfiction. Names, characters, places, and incidents are used factually, and any resemblance to actual persons, living or dead, is intentional.

For information, contact:
www.atlaselitepublishingpartners.com

All rights reserved worldwide. Printed in the United States of America.

Table of Contents

Introduction 1

Brooke Revuelta 3
The Next Generation

Carl Foster 10
Inside World Pickleball

Casey Brown 18
The Beauty of The Game

Chandler Carney 23
The Pickleball Ambassador

Chelsea Donovan 30
What's Your Story?

Danny Jensen 36
The Game of Life

Danny Wuerffel 44
From Pigskin to Pickleball

Darius Christian 48
The Pickleball Tour

Daryl Wyatt 54
Pickleball Down Under

Devin Alexander 61
The Pickleball Chef

Dustin and Lisa DeMeritt 66
Pickles and Dinky Balls

Emily Akradi 72
A Lifetime of Pickleball

Erica Desai and Mary Cannon 77
CityPickle

Ernie and Loida Medina 83
Pickleball for Life

Evan Slaughter 89
For the Fun of the Game

Geoff Nyugen 95
The Courts at Piccadilly

Gordon Gebert... 102
Rockin' on the Pickleball Court

Jared Bonner 109
Pickleheads

Jared Paul 115
The Kitchen

Jay "Gizmo" Hall 123
Pickleball Farm

Jodi Cullity 131
From Global Stages to Pickleball Courts

Joe Gannascoli 138
Pickleball Mafia

Joy Macci 143
Joy of Pickleball

Julie Scott 150
Order on the Court!

Kaitlin Miller 156
The Voice of Pickleball

Kamryn Blackwood 166
From DUPR Girl to Broadcaster on PBTV

Kelli Alldredge 175
Chicken and Pickle

Lieve Olivera 181
A "Special" Game

Marianne Orr 187
Champion of the Chair

Martina Kochli 193
American Pickleball

Matt Manasse 200
Pickleball Coach to the Stars

Mattias Johannson 208
The Pickleball OG

Megan Fudge 215
A Family Affair

Mehvish Safdar 222
The Doctor of Pickleball

Michael "Sleeves" Sliwa 227
Pickleball Maniac

Mick Tingstrom 234
A Game of Giving

Noah Suemnick 240
Faith in Pickleball

Paul Olson 245
A Man, A Van and a Plan

Rick Barry 253
All Star of Pickleball

Riley Palmer 260
The Queen of Pickleball

Sandy Halkett 265
Adaptive Pickleball

Scott Moore 270
The Ageless Wonder

Stephanie Lane 278
A Center Court Memory

Tara Fieri 283
Passion for Pickleball

Timber Tucker 289
The Pickleball Jacket

Wilbur Matthews 295
Portside Pickle

Acknowledgements 301
About the Author 302

Introduction

I'll be the first to admit it. For years, I snickered at pickleball players as we walked around them to play our regular weekend tennis game. Like most, I thought the game looked silly and even pathetic. Why in the world would anyone stop playing tennis to hit some dinky little plastic ball? I just couldn't figure it out. And quite honestly, I didn't care.

Fast forward to 2022. I'm in Sarasota, Florida, playing a mixed doubles tennis game. It wasn't a tournament, but our opponents acted like it was. I'll spare the details and only say that what happened that evening not only caused me to take a break from the game, but also was the impetus for my pickleball journey to begin.

Even after that, I was not thinking that pickleball was even a thing. A friend and I dropped in for open play at a YMCA, having just bought paddles the night before at Walmart. We stepped on the basketball court, play began, and I was hooked!

Since then, I sold my tennis rackets and have never looked back. It's a game that offers so much. I've played pickleball from Maine to Florida. In wind and rain, from freezing temps to heat that is sometimes unbearable. I've forgotten more game scores and more bad shots than I care to discuss. And what I remember are the laughs, the great stories, the random friendships, the beautiful courts, and the open communities.

The Pickleball Effect is my attempt at sharing what we all experience in this game. The community didn't disappoint me, with so many offering to share their stories. My only hope is that you have as much fun reading this book as I did writing it.

Brooke Revuelta

The Next Generation

In the spring of 2023, while still in the middle of her high school tennis season, Brooke Revuelta made a discovery that would change the trajectory of her life.

"I started playing pickleball recreationally with a friend. At first, I was just looking for something fun and casual outside of tennis, because tennis can be a little frustrating. So, I found pickleball."

What began as a lighthearted distraction quickly became a daily obsession. Before long, she was playing pickleball more than tennis—much to her high school tennis coaches' dismay.

"Our coaches didn't like that, but they had to deal with it," she said.

Despite the conflict, Brooke, a junior in high school at the time, helped her varsity tennis team win a state championship that year. After that victory, she turned her full focus to pickleball.

"I jumped into a pro tournament five months after learning how to play and never looked back."

From that moment on, pickleball became the center of Brooke's world. Her training regimen is relentless.

"I have one, two, maybe even three practice sessions a day. I usually like to drill more than I play. So, it's either one or two drill sessions a day. And then I'll have games a couple of times a week. But honestly, I love drilling way more. I get more out of it."

In addition to court time, she trains several times a week in the gym with her personal trainer. "That's basically my life. I eat, breathe, and sleep pickleball right now."

Beyond her rapid rise in the sport, one of the most rewarding aspects of Brooke's pickleball journey has been international travel.

In January 2025, she traveled to India to compete on a team at the World Pickleball League—and soon after in March 2025, she was selected for a goodwill pro pickleball military tour coordinated by Armed Forces Entertainment in association with Pro Sports MVP Entertainment & Promotions.

"Pickleball has taken me to so many new places across the U.S and around the globe that I don't think I would have ever gone. Like when I went to India earlier this year and did a goodwill professional pickleball military tour across Europe with a few other professional players."

As the granddaughter of three generations of military veterans, the opportunity held personal meaning.

"The first time I visited a military base was surreal. We stayed in the barracks, walked everywhere on the bases, and participated in the daily routines. It opened my eyes to a whole new world," Brooke said.

Alongside pros Danny Jensen and Taylor Garcia, Brooke traveled across Europe, visiting 12 U.S. military bases, bringing joy to troops through the sport she loves. "We visited U.S. military bases to boost troop morale and spread the love of the sport. It was amazing!"

The pros ran clinics, hosted exhibition matches, and played in mixed matchups with soldiers. "We had a lot of 'play with or against the pro' sessions where they would try to beat us or play with us against another amateur and a pro and battle it out. It was a lot of fun. Everybody enjoyed it."

The experience forged unexpected friendships.

"I have a couple of soldiers that I've stayed in contact with. I just talked to one the other day."

She continues to hear stories of games that still go on, long after the pros have left.

"It's so great to hear or watch them play pickleball after we leave and keep growing the sport."

One particularly unforgettable moment happened at a base in Kosovo.

"The troops were rooting for us to beat up on their Commander. It was hilarious! They thought beating us would be easy. Of course, it never happened."

On that goodwill tour, Brooke's passport collected stamps from Germany, Italy, Kosovo, Macedonia, Spain, Turkey, and the U.K.—a testament to how far the sport is taking her, both literally and professionally.

Now a second-year member of the APP Next Gen National Team, Brooke is firmly planted in her professional journey.

"I'm still working to rise up those ranks. I only play on the APP Tour right now."

Her approach to tournaments reflects a mature mindset rarely seen in athletes her age.

"I don't try to put any expectations on myself, in my game, or in my tournament results, just so it's not like an unrealistic standard or anything. But every time I go out there, I'm trying to play my best, play my game. If I lose, I want to lose playing my game, not beating myself," she said.

Pickleball has completely altered Brooke's life path. She was once headed to college on a D1 tennis scholarship last year. Now, she's chasing global podiums with a paddle.

"I've had a 180-degree change because I was supposed to play D1 college tennis out of my home state. Pickleball completely changed my life."

"You never know where it will take you. In June this year, I competed in Spain and in August I'm heading to play in England for a second year. I would have never thought that pickleball would take me to all these places – it will be 10 countries in the first eight months of 2025. It's been the best feeling."

When asked about her on-court demeanor, Brooke's dual personality shines through.

"I chill out and see what I see. I mean, when I get in the zone, I'm in the zone. But that's only on court for me. Off court, pickleball is such a social sport. You can walk up to anybody and start having a conversation and playing. The sport is so inviting," she said.

"There are all these groups of people you get invited to play with, and people are a lot more inviting and welcoming. That's what people love about it. You can just hop in, and anybody's going to welcome you. And you'll make friends on the court too."

She even helped a young woman stationed in Germany find her community. "I met a girl in Germany who had just moved there and was living on base, so it was a little bit harder for her to find friends. I told her to join a pickleball group right away, because of how easy it would be to meet new people."

When asked what she thinks fans love most, Brooke doesn't hesitate.

"I think one thing fans love is the underdog winning. And if it's broadcast on more streaming services, more people will watch the sport."

Still, she acknowledges the sport has room to grow on-screen.

"On screen makes the game look a lot slower. But I think the APP and PPA are doing a great job to promote and show the game."

She sees the power of star athletes and social media driving the sport's growth.

"I think having pro athletes involved, like getting Andre Agassi to play with Anna Leigh has helped bring more attention to the game."

Brooke herself is a fan of content that blends humor and culture.

She said, "@memesofpickleball is the best page. The guy who runs it is very on it, and he has the funniest ones of them all. I think he watches every single match ever and finds the littlest things to put on there. It's hilarious!"

She knows appearances matter, too.

She said, "You see girls put on a cute pickleball outfit and then snap a picture for social media. It's growing the sport, because somebody wants that outfit to play pickleball in."

"And it's even in commercials, like the Super Bowl one with Paris Todd and Hunter Johnson. That's insane! But it's just another example of the opportunities that pickleball will bring you."

Brooke has a sharp eye on the next generation.

She said, "I used to go to my local park every single night, religiously, and play with people older than me. There are so many younger people playing now who are in their teens and twenties. The youth are the key to the growth of the sport, especially the younger kids who get into it now, like 10 to 12 years old. By the time they're in college, they should have pickleball in the NCAA as a scholarship sport."

She sees a few logistical hurdles ahead.

"From the scholarship standpoint, they have to figure it out, because the coed part of it is a little bit tricky. They have to get around that."

But she's optimistic.

"With so many clubs already, and the number of younger kids playing continuing to increase, scholarship programs will attract great players."

As far as she's concerned, pickleball has no downside.

"When you think pickleball, you think fun. You don't think anything negative. I just can't find one thing," she said.

For young players looking to follow in her footsteps, Brooke offers practical advice with passion.

She said, "You just have to do it and throw yourself into the game. It's the best way you're going to learn and get better. Find some pros who will play with you."

"When you go to professional tournaments, you'll get that match play and see the level that you need to be playing at. And if you do it repeatedly, you get better. If you're consistent with it, and with the stuff you do outside of tournaments, you will get better."

Finding the right mentor matters.

"If you can find a coach who is strictly a pickleball player, do it. That helped me the most. Drilling and having a coach that didn't have a tennis background, just someone who knew the game of pickleball, was huge. He taught me the fundamentals and walked me through the baby steps. That was the best thing for me."

So what drives her love for the game?

"I love it because of the community, the energy, and the challenge. It's got a fun side, but it also has its competitive edge. I love the balance of competitiveness and fun, and joy in the sport. Pickleball welcomes anybody, at any age. The first people I ever played against were over age 50 or 60. It's truly a beautiful game that brings everybody together."

Carl Foster

Inside World Pickleball

"Five years ago, I was working with the Delray Beach ATP tennis tour and have been the voice of that for twenty-nine years."

The Baron family (who owns that tournament) called to ask what I knew about pickleball.

"I said, I never even heard of it. The family told me I needed to study up on it because they were going to host a tournament and wanted me to do a 30-minute TV special up at the Port St. Lucie complex at PGA, Verano."

Only six months before the event, Carl started researching the game.

"I went to my first event, and there were 250 players and some pros, in attendance, like Steve Kennedy and Rob Cassidy."

Carl couldn't believe what he was seeing.

"Where have I been, and where did this sport come from?"

He started interviewing top industry executives and players, and then one thing led to another.

"One of my initial interviews was with Melissa McCurley, who was like the first lady of pickleball and running tournaments."

Carl asked if anybody was doing TV shows with pickleball. He was told no, and they asked him for help.

He said, "I had done Inside Florida Tennis and the Tennis Magazine TV shows for probably over a decade. I also did Inside Golf and the Golf Magazine show that aired on Fox Sports nationally and then all the regional sports channels for years."

Carl decided to launch Inside Florida Pickleball in 2020. His first pickleball interviews were with Anna Lee Waters and Leigh Waters, who lived locally in Delray Beach, and had just won the U.S. Open National Championships as a mother/daughter team (Anna Leigh was only 12).

Shot at the end of the pandemic, it was the first time most had come out of their house.

"We didn't want to get too close to anybody, so we had masks on, and I interviewed them across the net."

Carl didn't start playing until this new TV show.

He said, "I was still playing tennis and golf. And then I met Steve Kennedy, who is now a Hall of Famer. And he asked if I wanted to do Tips of the Week with Steve Kennedy? So, we started doing tips and got his paddle company, Engage, to sponsor it."

He also explains his journey in Pickleball.

"I tried an Engage paddle and was hooked after the first lesson, and being a competitive tennis player, the game came to me pretty quickly. I was playing tennis with my pickleball paddle for a while trying to figure out the strategy, and the rest is history. It's been an amazing pickleball journey.

At 73, Carl is still competing, winning several medals.

"Almost every day I'm out playing on the courts in Boca Raton," he said.

Carl then expanded Inside World Pickleball, taking it national.

"Fox Sports picked up the show for the first year. Then I did a 13-week series with CBS Sports and Inside World Pickleball. That's when I teamed up with the APP and I started my first tournament, which was the Delray Beach Pickleball Open."

He continues, "They had eight pickleball courts, and we transferred the stadium court into four pickleball courts. We got CBS to do the finals and ended up having 27 total courts and almost one thousand players with top pros like Anna Leigh Waters and Ben Johns."

Living in Boca Raton, Carl wanted to host a pickleball tourney locally at the Patch Reef Tennis Center. Well connected to the city and the tennis community since 1983, he knew it would work.

"There was no PPA tour, as they were just getting rolling. The APP was partnered with Ken Herman, so we teamed it up for the first year, then bought back the rights from the APP Tour," he said.

"My partner is actually a Purple Heart Navy SEAL veteran, whom I have known for over 25 years. We reconnected through Pickleball about five years ago."

Now in its 5th year, The Boca Masters has attracted more than 5,000 players.

"We transitioned the tennis facility into 36 courts with a nice stadium. Our event has always been sanctioned by USA Pickleball, but I'm not affiliated with any of the pro tours. But I do get pros to play through our partnership with the NPL and the Senior Pro Tour," Carl said.

Carl is excited for the growth of the game and how it's helping others.

He said, "I'm a military vet, so I work a lot with the veterans, and I'm seeing a lot of the guys that have just been stagnant with PTSD, other injuries, and health issues, able to get back out and get some exercise with pickleball."

He continues, "You can pick up the game pretty easily. The beauty of the sport is I could give you a lesson of five minutes and you can be out there hitting the ball with your kids, your grandkids or your wife or spouse. And that's why it's exploding because it's the ease of entry."

In 2024, Carl started a 501c3 called the Veterans Pickleball Association, knowing it was the right time.

"I was playing with more veterans and first responders during the pandemic and got to know a lot of them."

With their first tournament, he got DUPR to sponsor the event, and veterans helped staff it.

Known as the Veterans Pickleball Tour, Carl has aligned with several organizations like Camp Hope PTSD Foundation (https://ptsdusa.org/camp-hope/), Military Adaptive Sports, and the VA.

Carl said, "I met one of the guys who runs the only Houston complex who's a military vet. He told me that they want to add pickleball to the facility, so we raised enough funds for them to buy some nets and start a fund to build a new court on site."

Pickleball is helping veterans get back into the community.

"People are respecting them for being veterans, no matter what size or shape they're in or how old they are. And they're able to go out there and compete again, even in tournaments. That's the beauty of it," Carl explained.

Since picking up pickleball, Carl's competitive juices have started flowing again.

"I started to play 2-3 hours every day with a group of players here in Boca. It's keeping me active and in shape. And I feel bad if I don't go out and play first thing in the morning because it's a morning ritual. I'm up at six o'clock. I'm out on the courts by seven."

Carl recently acquired a 50% stake in the Boca Raton Rattlers (a 50+ league) with long-time friend Rick Retamar.

He said, "In 2024, we won both the regular season and the NPL Championship Playoffs. The mayor gave us the key to the city, as we were the first pro team in Boca Raton to win a National Title."

This past year, his team proudly led the Holiday Parade.

"It's just the relationships we've built and seeing people, all different age groups. One of my good friends I play with is 75 years old. I love to play with younger people too, and use pickleball to stay in shape and stay healthy."

"The growth of the sport is recreational," he said, "It's the younger generation coming up. And it's also the seniors."

Carl has seen a resurgence in the 50 and 60-plus age groups.

"Pickleball has mobilized the seniors back into their heyday of competition, which has added in travel. And then there's all these ladies that really didn't have a chance to do things in a lot of their lives. And now they are playing the game, and they can have competitions."

Carl also sees more leagues that are starting now.

"Down in Florida, you've got all these country clubs that have pickleball courts now. The tennis leagues we used to play in have become pickleball leagues. I know of a Boca's women's league with 700 players. They're all decked out in their uniforms, and they're all getting together."

One morning, Carl had just finished playing. "We always say, 'here come the Housewives of Boca,' because they show every morning at 9 a.m. They just take over the courts."

A favorite pickleball story of Carl's features NBA player Jason Williams.

He said, "I didn't really know him before, even though I had worked in the NBA for the Cleveland Cavaliers. But I knew the name."

Carl explained he was playing at a four-court facility in Boca Raton when a really tall guy walked in.

"So, I said, who the heck is that? It's gotta be a basketball player. Turns out a friend of mine who was a doctor, was actually working with Jason at a treatment center for athletes."

After hitting that morning, Carl built a friendship and has since participated in some of Jason's foundation events.

"On Florida courts, you will often see players from the NBA, NFL, MLB, and even the NHL," He said.

Carl even met the Mayor of Boca Raton on the courts one day.

"He comes out to all my tournaments. He promotes my tournaments. He supports them. He says pickleball is great for the city of Boca."

Carl tells the veterans to get out often.

"I tell them to grab a paddle and go out to the courts. This is the new networking platform of the world because you will not move as fast through this world as you will with pickleball. For some reason, our guard is down, our happiness is up, the community is there, the competition's on, and everyone is the same person."

He said, "It's so much faster than the golf days where you joined a club and played, but nothing like pickleball where I can be pretty close to someone after the first game."

He continues, "It's the ease of getting into the sport. I mean, with golf and tennis, you've got to take some lessons before you can even play the game, let alone meet somebody and be competitive on that level."

Carl loves the simplicity of the game, and the ease of interaction.

He said, "I can go to any court here, any public court, just walk in, put my paddle in, meet new people, and just go out and start playing. You want to mix up and start at different levels. You want to try to play. You want to play competitive games. I'll even teach new players."

"My first couple of games might be with two or three ladies who can hardly hit the ball over the net. But you know what they say? We need a fourth. I never say no."

For Carl, the family connection to pickleball is strong.

"I taught my son Chase to play as he grew up with tennis and is now 25," Carl said.

"Both Chase and my ballerina daughter Carla couldn't figure out what I was doing for a while. But being athletic, they picked it up quickly and got hooked right away. And now my daughter's playing up in New York and my son's playing up in Palm Beach," he said.

Chase works at Christ Fellowship Church, and the pastors and staff are all playing.

"It's amazing, as the Christian community has just exploded with Pickleball."

He said Pickleball is a sport that brings people together.

"Most or all of the people I've met over the last five years have been through pickleball. Now they're all my friends. We get together, we watch football games together, we go out to parties together. Our kids get married, and we go to weddings together. We travel together now. And we only travel if there are pickleball courts. It's a great blessing and a chance to be competitive again on this pickleball journey."

Casey Brown

The Beauty of The Game

While attending a weekend retreat for Inspiring Children in Las Vegas, NV, Casey was introduced to the game of pickleball.

"I grew up playing tennis and had never heard of the game. But one of the activities that week was pickleball, so I gave it a try."

She had a blast but gave the game no more thought until the pandemic happened.

"We were a few weeks into lockdown, and I was in Nashville. It was a tough time, as I had to cancel all my events, and a friend passed away at a young age due to cancer," she said.

While Casey battled with a new schedule, a pause in work, and new habits, her sleep schedule became unhealthy.

"All my friends were waking up every morning and playing pickleball. But I still wasn't interested."

As the pandemic moved into March, Casey watched more and more of her friends play the game. Her mind started to realize the connection through this game.

"The reason that I love pickleball is that it brought people together during a really hard time from different backgrounds. I saw some of my celebrity friends, entrepreneurs, musicians, and people of all walks of life on the courts with one another."

"Nobody knew who the other was, and I just thought that was a beautiful thing."

This new life experience inspired Casey to come up with the idea of The Necker Island Pickleball Forum.

"Pickleball to me has always been more than just a sport," she said.

While she appreciates the competitive level, Casey knew that pickleball is about bringing people together on and off the court.

"I've seen it help a lot of people through really hard times."

Working with many celebrities, Casey has heard stories from many about how the game has fundamentally changed them. Often an outlet from chaotic lives, most find pickleball as a way to escape from reality and enjoy the simplicity of the game.

Close to the Drew Brees Foundation, Casey has seen an amazing influence in New Orleans.

She said, "Drew brings the community together during summer, and he throws a huge pickleball event, and it does so much good for the community. They put together an incredible weekend of pickleball for the community and for those who come in from out of state."

It's been events like this that changed her perspective.

Says Casey, "I realized how it shifted everything and how people were playing in their backyards or just creating courts. It's everywhere you go."

Casey knows how special pickleball can be. The game starts the conversation, the conversation starts the camaraderie, and the camaraderie starts the community.

"I think lots of deep conversations come from pickleball because of how small the court is, and how you can sit down and talk afterwards. Everyone seems to extend their pickleball to breakfast, to lunch, and to dinner."

Casey recognizes the community of the game.

"I just think that's beautiful," she said.

Watching the industry inspired Casey to create something on Necker Island.

"I knew I wanted to do another event of some sort on Necker. And I had the privilege to be a partner of Premier Live whose team had built the Necker Cup, which is going on for the 14th year."

Next year, The Necker Island Pickleball Forum will host its third event.

"It's been such a success," she said. "We are building seven courts and bringing ten pros. I love bringing people together and watching the musicians, athletes, and pros play with our other guests. I mean, that's the essence of Necker Island, what Richard's built; Pickleball, music, Necker Island."

"I think that music ties people together as well. We have also invited TV personalities, comedians, and celebrity chefs," says Casey.

"Everyone keeps asking me, *why do you do it?* And I'm like, it's to bring people together. Also, it's been a very healing journey for me and many others!"

Casey's duties during the event don't often give her the time to experience it.

"I'll be floating around managing things. The craziest part for me is when I depart the island and realize the friendships that were created from the event."

"I have produced many events, and the ones here always bring out the kindness in people," she said.

"It's really cool to see who's meeting up, and in what city. You could be in California, Florida, Minnesota, wherever. And that is so cool to me. One of our musicians could be on tour somewhere and catch up with another guest in Texas. This is what builds friendships."

In Nashville, there's a rooftop pickleball court called Dinkville at the Bobby Hotel.

Casey said, "A lot of the people who were playing during the 2020 pandemic are now playing up on that roof. During the summer in Nashville, that's a really big thing to go play on the rooftop where they even host celebrity events and pro-ams."

She continues,

"I think pickleball is kind of similar to the yoga movement in some ways, if you think about it and how it helps clear the mind," she says.

"And the game is so easily accessible. I do personally believe that pickleball is for the good."

Casey sees the sport really growing in the urban areas.

"I'd really like to see a lot more of the game to help kids get off their phones."

For Casey, pickleball is fun to see and watch.

"Even if you're not playing an actual game, you're going to be okay because you can just dink wherever you want, and that's pretty fun."

"Have you seen that Instagram channel (@cafricapickleball)?" Casey asked. "I think it's this group in Africa that's playing pickleball. It's like these kids and everyone. They are so happy and there's so much joy there. And you can tell that it's like a daily thing."

A lot of Casey's pickleball friends follow the channel, and she hopes to see more Instagram pages from other parts of the world.

Casey has seen pickleball change lives all around her.

"One of my best friends was dealing with some tough personal issues. Now that she plays pickleball all the time, she is a different person. It has changed her life. I think she's just happier, as it's given her a purpose.

Even my dad, who has always played tennis, has picked up the game," she said.

"And my eighty-eight-year-old grandmother can dink the ball. She loves to play pickleball."

Chandler Carney
The Pickleball Ambassador

Looking back, Chandler remembers first seeing pickleball in high school.

She said, "Back in 2006, my gym class teacher introduced us to the sport but not as we know it now."

We used wooden paddles, but we all loved it. It was fast paced, but I did not view it as a competitive sport at the time."

In 2013, Chandler was visiting Chile while doing an internship and fell in love with the country.

"I saw this work-life balance and really great weather," she said.

Now calling it home, she soon helped to start the "Chile Movement" for pickleball.

"When I later moved to Chile full-time, I found a paddle and immediately fell in love with it," she said.

The game activated Chandler's dominant competitive side, getting her back into athletic clothing and allowing her to go slam the ball.

She said, "I started training every day and ended up joining Team USA to play in the Pan-American games in Paraguay and later in Brazil."

"During the pandemic, we had a lucky break where we finally traveled," says Chandler.

She went back to Naples, Florida to be with family and started searching for padel games.

"There were no padel courts to be found, and all I kept hearing about was pickleball."

Chandler decided to check out what all the hype was about.

"At the time, I had played so much padel and other athletic activities that I had an overuse injury to my wrist."

Not wanting to lose the progress she had made in paddle, Chandler decided to stay moving through pickleball, despite a recent wrist operation.

"At first, I started writing to people on Facebook asking where I could play." She was directed to a local park with courts and was immediately invited into a game. "They lent me a paddle, and they taught me how to play. I was initially lost with the scoring but eventually caught on."

In her very first game, Chandler won playing with her opposite hand.

"The players were shocked to discover I wasn't actually left-handed! We had a lot of fun. I came away from that moment ready to go all-in on pickleball."

On her return to Chile, Chandler struggled to find a place to play.

"There wasn't much going on with pickleball at the time. My first game in Chile was actually in a parking garage."

With hardly any dedicated clubs or competition, Chandler and her business partner decided to ignite pickleball in Chile.

"We found places to host clinics, even if that meant taping court lines on gym floors or tennis courts. We convinced friends from padel to come and try out the sport. Once they tried it, they were hooked," she said.

"The kids really do love it. The lighter paddle weight and smaller paddle size really make it an ideal sport for them. They can truly compete with parents, coaches, etc.," she said.

"At the ATP Chile Open, we put on an incredible clinic with the ball boys and girls, all of whom took to the sport immediately due to their strong background in racquet sports. Some of them played so well they ended up challenging their tennis coaches right then and there and winning!"

She said, "I think it's a highly accessible sport, which is what makes it really so attractive. It's low-cost. Pickleball can be set up on any hard, flat surface. You put the tape down and set up a portable net."

Chandler also had the honor of putting on a clinic at the Chilean Olympic Center, a moment that will forever stay with her as pickleball continues on its Olympic-recognition journey.

"Chile is a very strong racket sports country. Tennis culture is strong and Padel broke records within the nation," she said.

With padel courts on nearly every corner, she doesn't see the sport as competition.

Says Chandler, "Instead, we see more people than ever in the history of the country playing a racket sport. The transition over to pickleball comes naturally to them."

The local market has embraced the sport.

She said, "The CEO of a large hotel chain in Chile is very interested in how to connect the sport with tourism. And I think he's going to be a key person in helping promote this and possibly even install courts at specific tourist locations like country clubs and wineries."

In the last two years, Chandler has helped to grow the sport to new heights in Chile.

She co-founded the largest club to date, Pickleball UC by KONDOR, and played on the Chilean national team in 2023 and 2024.

She recently helped form the Chilean Pickleball Association, inspired by her role as a board member of the Global Pickleball Federation.

"I wanted to bring my way of thinking as a lawyer and an athlete to pickleball. I had witnessed first-hand what happens when a sport lacks democratic and transparent governance principles, and that is the last thing I wanted for pickleball."

Globally speaking, Chandler sees a movement.

"It's on every cruise ship. I even got a friend of mine here in Chile teaching pickleball on cruise ships. So, he's very pleased."

She continues, "I think other countries are lucky in that they have the U.S. as a pioneer and as a point of reference in all of this."

Chandler knows we can learn and accelerate the process of implementing pickleball on a national level in each of these countries, turning to the United States and its resources.

She said, "We've got a lot of resources to play with. It's going to be very global. The game is going to probably change eventually. And the pickleball that we know, we have seen that change already."

Chandler has seen things like ball speed and power elevate.

"That's where the Federation will come in, and we'll have to put a cap on that power. Because if you don't, you lose the quality of the game. You lose those rallies that we love so much and that people want to go see."

She said, "Agassi has been such a benefit to the game, and a huge influence around the world. He's traveled to India, and I believe to China as well. He's just really been out there as a superstar tennis player. He is now pickleball's biggest advocate."

Chandler continues, "After the Pickleball Slam, we noticed on Google trends an uptick in people searching the term pickleball in Chile. So, there's no doubt that the celebrities getting involved has a giant influence on where the sport is going and getting other people to learn about the sport or motivate others to try the sport."

She said, "The Asian market is going to be huge. India is looking to host the 2036 Olympics. The Indian Pickleball Association was just recognized by the Ministry of Sport in India as the official federation. So, they're moving very fast. They've got a lot of facilities. Vietnam and Malaysia have an insane amount of growth, and beautiful clubs. We will continue to see strong developments in Asia in the coming years."

Something that Chandler has talked about from the beginning is future opportunities for players at the collegiate level. She believes this will eventually be recognized as an NCAA sport.

"Right now, there is a collegiate club model, and some entities are putting together a collegiate championship."

She continues, "I would like to think that whenever a sport is recognized by the NCAA or where there exists an opportunity for a scholarship, that directly affects the interest and what people are doing in other countries because they see that opportunity. If you could get a full ride athletic scholarship playing pickleball in the United States, you're going to see that as an opportunity and train for pickleball in Chile."

"I really do feel like I have impacted people's lives through the sport and that's very rewarding to say the least."

Says Chandler," We had a lady come to open play who has a deformity in her spine. It's hard for her to move, she has mobility issues, so it's hard for her to run. We weren't sure exactly how to approach it at first because this was the first for us. I don't have specific training in para pickleball or adaptive pickleball, but I did know I had seen in rule books that adjustments can be made."

"So, they made one. They let the ball bounce twice. A small tweak, a big difference. She was grateful for that."

Chandler adds. "And honestly, it's been amazing to watch her take on the challenge in her own way. She's really had a great time playing with the group. Seeing her out there—smiling, improving, connecting—it's been a highlight for all of us."

She said, "I really do feel like I've made an impact in people's lives through this sport, and that's incredibly rewarding."

Last year, Chandler's club put together, for the first time ever, a senior team.

"The senior team has bonded. They're very close. They're a great group. We put together a meeting prior to the World Cup where they got together and they just ate, and they talked, and they got to know each other better."

One of the ladies on the team shared how she was recently widowed and had also lost a child.

"She was going through a really tough time emotionally, mentally. Pickleball became her outlet to distract herself and kind of be social again. It gave her something to look forward to and goals to work towards. And it truly made such a difference for her. Everyone was nearly in tears listening to her story and how it's changed her life."

Asked the most unique place Chandler has played pickleball, she responds, "I think that's an up-and-coming answer that it's going to be Greece and it's going to be in Olympia. On our trip, we will stay on a yacht and play on a floating pickleball court."

She continues, "I love pickleball because it ignites my competitive spirit and brings happiness to my life."

Chelsea Donovan

What's Your Story?

What started as a simple visit with her parents has turned into a full-blown sport of passion for Chelsea.

"I started playing the game with my parents' friends who were much older than me," she said.

Living in Wilmington, NC, Chelsea immediately fell in love with the game and started playing several times a week.

"My parents aren't playing as much as I am anymore. They are focusing on the grandparent thing," she said.

"During COVID, I was involved in a group in Hampton Roads that was itching to get into pickleball. We literally took a parking lot at a mall that they normally create into an ice-skating rink, and made it into four courts by taping the lines."

It immediately caught on, and even today, the courts are still there.

Say Chelsea, "People are still playing on asphalt. The beginners go out there at the mall and learn in the parking lot."

Now the lines are painted on the ground, and everyone brings their own nets.

"Every single person that I know, knows that I'm crazy about pickleball. I mean, everybody at the station that I work with, all my colleagues, all the anchors, they know."

When there's something that pops in her inbox about pickleball, Chelsea always gets it.

"They always send it to me. As a TV personality, and I have been for almost 25 years, they encourage you to post your personal life on your pages. It's been fun because I've been asked to play in little celebrity tournaments. And when I'm at the clubs, they think it's cool to play with someone from the media."

Chelsea said, "Whenever I pop on the court, no matter the day of the week, no matter where, people always want to discuss the news. We don't talk about anything but what I do. Because there are 2.8 million people who turn on their TV at night, and those are our viewers, it's helped build a bond because they see me on TV at four or five and then six o'clock. When I'm out there, we're always talking about the news of the day, which I think gives them that relationship, and I can just be open. They can ask questions, and it builds a really good rapport."

"I think one of the things that pickleball has that no other sport has is the social aspect," says Chelsea.

Whenever she travels, Chelsea gets on her phone to figure out where to play.

"I join Facebook groups, I show up all the time alone, and within five minutes you're sharing your story, you're making new friends, and you're exchanging phone numbers."

She loves the intimacy and feel of the community, whether it's a little town in Idaho or New York City.

Chelsea knows the game is not cliquey.

"I think that's why I like it, and why so many beginners do too. Everybody welcomes you with open arms in most places, whether you're an advanced competitive player or you've never picked up a paddle before."

She loves the inclusivity of pickleball and the feeling that you're part of something and welcomed, no matter who you are or what your background is.

One of her favorite stories of how pickleball changed the life of another is truly amazing.

Says Chelsea, "I've seen a guy that I play with all the time that was 500 or 600 pounds and is now down to 250."

Once an alcoholic and completely overweight, this player is now on the court seven days a week.

"He's out there when it's 90 degrees in a hooded sweatshirt, with a jacket over top of that. It's like he's training. He is such an amazing guy, and an amazing player."

Chelsea hears these stories often.

"No one tells them. I should strap on a Go Pro, mic up some people, and talk. Those are the best stories."

"So far, this industry has provided me with acceptance. You can be a really skilled Emmy award-winning journalist and be accepted and be able to talk to people in the pickleball industry and even CEOs of companies," she said.

Chelsea wants to take her skills, whether it be public speaking, writing, or storytelling, and dig deep to find stories that are untold.

"We hear so much about the celebrities and the new paddle and the courts opening. But I think there is an untapped part of pickleball that's aside from the pros, that's aside from the big tournaments, that's aside from the PPA, that really could lend itself to some really good stories."

She said, "When I moved to Raleigh in 2022, I was just going to the open play at six rough courts that were formerly tennis courts and sort of got my bearings there. This was before Raleigh had any indoor facility."

Chelsea got lots of practice and met a lot of people.

"Now that circle has expanded to hundreds of people because there are a couple of franchises here that have built three or four different indoor facilities. And I've become a member there."

Chelsea knows the friendships that she's made in the last two years are people she could call on at any point.

"It's not just pickleball. We meet outside of work, grab dinners, whatever. Pickleball was the impetus for how it all started."

Looking at her phone now, every name ends with "pickleball."

"It's really a blessing!"

"I got a good story for you," Says Chelsea. "Back when I started, there were some people that my parents were playing with that were very good competitive senior players, maybe 4.5s. I was new to the game, but I knew that I was younger and more athletic."

She continues, "There was a night that my parents and I and a couple of friends, had gone out to dinner and had some drinks. And I said to one of my parents' friends, who was a female in her late sixties, 'I'll take you on. I'll play singles with you tomorrow.' And I said, 'You're not going to win. I'm, 35 years old, I'm faster, and there's just no way that you can beat me.'"

The next morning, Chelsea woke up and stuck to her word.

"I went and met her out on the court. It was early in the morning, and I was dehydrated from the night before. So I played a few points and was getting my butt kicked. The next thing you know, I pop my calf muscle. You could just hear it burst."

Her opponent ran into the clubhouse.

"She got dill pickle juice and mustard to try to get the sodium content in there. Then the ambulance came. I went off into the hospital, and was in a cast and on crutches for two months. I think that speaks to the sport. Now I'll remember that story forever because I think that's just a good lesson learned and a funny one."

Chealsea said, "I love playing pickleball. I've played in Mexico, in all of the different islands, in Florida, even Arizona. Arizona's a favorite: I think that the weather is amazing, the people are so welcoming, and it's so cool to be playing in places like Sedona and be surrounded by the beautiful red rocks."

Chelsea, she is surrounded by fanatics like herself.

"I have several friends in Charlotte who are pickleball crazy people and have built two or three courts in their backyard. And that's always fun because there's no waiting, which is the best part. But to be able to sit and go play pickleball and grill out and go play pickleball some more ... I think the backyard thing is really fun and it's cool to be able to be invited to someone's house who's got that coveted pickleball court in their backyard," Chealsea said.

"I think that the game is so fun because you can make a whole day out of it."

Chelsea often shows up at her club on a weekend at 10 a.m.

"They've got a restaurant in there, they've got a bar in there, you might take a break, get something to eat, go back out on the court.

I love to meet new people, make some new friends, and play with some old friends. The next thing you know, it's 6 p.m. and you can't believe you played pickleball for eight hours."

She continues, " I think for so many people, it's that timeout, that stress reliever, that time to unwind and just simply be your authentic self. You get to be competitive. You get to laugh. You get the exercise. You get to have fun."

Watching the industry, she knows there is still an untapped market.

Chelsea said, "I watched the US Open the other day and saw very minimal coverage on the adaptive athletes. Their athleticism and being able to manipulate a wheelchair and play at the same time is amazing!"

Chelsea knows there is work to be done when it comes to the viewing audience.

"How do you get people to watch it? How do you get people to tune in? My parents aren't tuning into Pickleball TV. They're not tuning into the US Open. They're not tuning into MLP or PPA. It's only the diehard pickleball fans that are watching it."

She said, "What is it going to take to get visibility? To me, it's like a conundrum. I think about it all the time. Like what's stopping people? Do they think it's just kind of dumb? Do they think, what is this? Is this kind of like half tennis, half ping pong, half badminton? It's just, I think about it all the time to figure out what the recipe is to get more eyes on the sport."

Danny Jensen
The Game of Life

"I love pickleball because it's opened up doors in my life that I didn't even know were possible. It's changed my life completely," Danny said.

Danny's story begins on a very different court. A former Division 1 soccer player at Ohio State, his athletic career ended abruptly in 2016 following a major head injury.

Says Danny, "It kind of changed my path of getting away from athletics and more into just the regular world. I ended up taking a few jobs, trying to find my own path."

He wasn't looking for a new sport when pickleball found him.

"One of the very first games I ever played. I was a true 2.5 player. I didn't know the rules, didn't know how to score, didn't know how to hold a paddle in my hand as it was a foreign object to me."

Despite being a total beginner, Danny was honest with the group on the court.

"To this day, I'll be thankful for being welcomed onto the court."

That gesture stuck with him.

Danny goes back to those courts sometimes and plays with his original group.

"I often think about how these people brought me in, taught me the rules all in one game, and enjoyed a game with me all at once."

He continues, "It's hard to say that there are moments that change your life, but one game of pickleball genuinely changed mine. And it's pretty cool to look back on that and think, wow, what if I hadn't met those exact people? What if they didn't even take a chance?"

That small act of inclusion has impacted Danny's life more than they'll ever know.

Danny recalls the day he found pickleball in 2021.

"I remember it was the day after July 4th. I was like, fine, I'll go play."

He had seen pickleball before but had never paid much attention to the sport.

"I just went and slapped a ball around for like 30 minutes to an hour. And that wasn't really like actually learning pickleball."

But something clicked. The next morning, he was back at the courts before sunrise.

"They start playing at 5:30 am, before the heat, and I just started playing."

It didn't take long for him to understand why people are obsessed with the sport.

"I like how you get feedback on your play. It helped fuel me to get better."

The real turning point came after reading a book that encouraged him to follow what he enjoyed.

"It's the one book that kind of changed my life. It was basically telling me to quit my job. And so I was like, okay, it makes sense."

Having saved up some money, Danny made a bold decision.

"I decided to just go play pickleball and go tour and play some tournaments and get my name out there and see how it goes."

What started as a six-month experiment turned into a two-year odyssey and eventually led him to become the founder of Paddle and Passport, a luxury travel company that now hosts curated pickleball experiences around the world.

"I essentially just played every day and got very, very obsessed with it, like almost borderline too obsessed, to the point where people were telling me to slow down or I was gonna get hurt."

He laughs, "I wouldn't have it any other way. It was the greatest decision of my life to pursue pickleball and go after something that maybe most people wouldn't have gone after. But hey, I'm here, I'm living proof that it's possible, and yeah, I'm still obsessed with pickleball to this day."

Coming from soccer, Danny had no racket sport background before he started to play.

"I understood how to use my feet, and that was about it. When I came into pickleball, I had such an appreciation for this hand-eye coordination that all these guys had. It's really amazing."

Even though the skills were hard-earned, he genuinely enjoyed the learning process.

"I don't necessarily think it's that crazy because we have a lot of movement in soccer."

He says, "A lot of core positioning comes from my soccer days. But the actual racket sport background is something that I just wish I always had. Now I look at my parents all the time and I'm like, 'You guys didn't want to put me into tennis? I'd be a lot better pickleball player right now if you guys would have done that.' So, I blame them for some of my shortcomings in pickleball," he jokes.

Cross-training is a big part of Danny's routine.

"I lift weights, I go for walks, and do a bunch of basic workouts. It helps me to clear my mind, to step away, and to stay grounded."

Now that pickleball is the center of his life, he admits it's not as relaxing as it once was.

"It's given me a world of experiences. Literally."

He said, "I have been able to travel to over 25 countries, with most of them through my three military tour adventures."

Being on tour has changed the way Danny sees the sport and the people in it.

"As much as these guys seem like individuals, everybody has teams around them. They have their best friends, because you realize quickly when you're on the road 26 to 36 weeks a year, you better find friends," he said.

"You better find a community that supports you. You better find a backbone when you're having your tough days."

That sense of belonging, of tribe, is something he's always valued.

"On the road, we play lots of card games," says Danny. "I'm amazed how our players are some of the most intellectual people I've ever met in my life. They get outrageously competitive over cards, and it carries over the next day to ping pong, or golf. We can't get ourselves away from the competition."

It's part of what keeps the fire alive.

"How does the viewing experience get better?" Danny asks. "I think that there are different camera angles that are more likely to show the actual skills. Even in tennis, it's hard to see that true speed from certain distances. When you see someone take a full wind-up and crush a ball at them, and they're able to react to it and counter the ball as hard as they can back, that's very difficult to portray to a viewer."

"But I think people would love the mic'd up version of some of these matches. I mean, some of them are friends versus friends," he says. "But when you get a few people that are trash-talking, there's no sport more entertaining than pickleball at the highest level."

Of course, fame brings its quirks.

Danny says, "There is a term on the tour we use called 'pickleball famous,' There's an issue right now with people's heads getting a little bit too big. They are 'pickleball famous,' so they walk around a venue and they feel like they are a star actor, and then they take that out of the venue."

He's quick to bring it back to what really matters.

"You've got to take it for what it's worth. But at the end of the day, we're not going to see exponential growth by ourselves. We have to have a community around us. We've got to have the world around us. So exponential growth comes with these people coming, leading the charge and being influential in this space."

Danny's next project is a reality TV show.

"It's more like a competition TV show," says Danny. "I was one of 16 players who got selected in a group of eight guys, and eight girls. It ended up being just like a week of filming, which was outrageously fun. I've met some amazing friends from the show."

He can't reveal much yet, but Danny's excited.

"The social proof has yet to come because it hasn't been aired yet, but I think that we're going to be excited with the results. All 16 people are going to have a lot of face time on the show. It's going to be very fun to see where it takes us."

Beyond the tour, Danny's proudest moments have come through his work with the military.

"Every week, someone is coming up to me, asking if I remember so-and-so from grade school, or telling me they know my cousin."

But his best stories are from the military bases.

"Some of the soldiers send clips of them watching my tournament games online. And this is while they are on base in places like Kuwait or Qatar."

"To take time out of their day and watch me from halfway across the world when it's the middle of the night for them is truly humbling."

Danny is never surprised when he is asked questions about a certain point, or why he made a shot one way.

"I respond to every single email. I love having the support of our troops overseas."

Through his tours teaching pickleball on military bases, Danny has seen firsthand the power of the game.

"Pickleball is a great addition to the bases. So many of our soldiers are going through tough times, and it helps to create a sense of community."

He continues, "Seeing them come together, regardless of rank, was amazing. It provides a temporary escape from reality. And on the pickleball court, there is no rank."

"I've seen them play on just about every surface you possibly can imagine, from asphalt to parking lots, to hangars where they'll move out their helicopters or planes. Even the fire departments will move the trucks out and play in there."

One of Danny's favorite stories happened in Saudi Arabia.

"A court was built out of parts that you would use for a runway. They painted lines on it. Then one of the guys with the electrical team brought lights that are used for the runway, and they lit the court."

Danny continues, "They put that all together to create an environment where everybody could play. It was quite fascinating to see the creativity used."

On another trip, Danny was challenged by members of the Explosive Ordnance Disposal (EOD) unit.

"They asked me how badly I thought I could actually beat them if I tried my best. So, I told them I would put on a bomb suit and play two-on-one. I wasn't being cocky, it was all in good fun," Danny says.

Then he laughs, "They accepted the challenge, I put the suit on and beat them handily."

Moments like these remind Danny what really matters.

"These guys are so excited to see us, even though we are not something like a famous band."

Danny continues, "When they hear 'pickleball pros,' they come in waves. They're competitive, and they really want to beat you. But then you realize, they're the ones making the ultimate sacrifice. They're the ones that are giving everything for me to be able to play this sport."

"It's so easy for me to be thankful for what I have after I get to see what they're doing for a living. I know a lot of them enjoy it, but I know many are also going through tough times. So, someone like me, when I get to be there, I actually enjoy it more than they do. And I hope that they realize that."

Danny Wuerffel

From Pigskin to Pickleball

"It was during COVID, and I was just looking for something to do," says Danny Wuerffel.

"At the time, my oldest son was in high school and had played some pickleball, so we went down to the local park. It was a fun thing to do together, and I just fell in love with it right away."

Wuerffel grew up training for football and basketball through high school.

"For fun, I played tennis, ping pong, and racquetball. My dad was a great racquetball player who also loved pickleball. My sister still plays national racquetball tournaments."

What hooked him was the strategy.

"As you get better, it's a lot more strategic than people think, which I love as a former quarterback, especially doubles."

He also values how inclusive it is.

"You can be an old man, a woman, super athletic, or not very athletic, and still have fun. Anyone can enjoy it pretty quickly. It's like a video game with a thousand levels. You can always get better, and there's always somebody better than you," he said.

Although pickleball was once seen as a sport for seniors, Wuerffel points to its rapid growth among younger players.

"My sons are playing at the University of Florida and in high school. At the US Open, the number of juniors competing was amazing. Young people are falling in love with the sport too, and the growth is incredible."

He has also noticed a generational shift.

"A lot of teenage boys today lack overall physical coordination, maybe because they spend more time on video games than playing outside. But their hand-eye coordination is incredible. I've seen kids who walk around like a baby giraffe about to fall over, but you can't hit a ball past them because their hand speed and reactions are so good."

Most of Wuerffel's playing happens at the Atlanta Pickleball Center with his "day-to-day crew."

"I played the full season last year in the National Pickleball League for Denver and had a great year. At the US Open, I made some good runs in the senior pro division. With almost 60 teams, it was kind of like March Madness."

His team made it to the Elite Eight, and he is gearing up for another season with the Denver Iconics.,

For Wuerffel, the community aspect is just as rewarding as the competition.

"My dad will go to the local courts, where there are six courts and maybe 50 people. They'll all be there for three or four hours getting to know everybody," he said.

He loves the social nature of the game compared with tennis or other sports.

"You're close enough to talk and have fun during matches."

That sense of community has led to stories he treasures.

"There's a woman named Renee at my dad's courts. She used to be heavier, but now she has lost so much weight. She wears bling, even on her paddle, and challenges everyone to singles. Ben Johns could show up, and she would still want to play him."

Another story is about a close friend from Puerto Rico.

"He came to America for his chiropractic degree but moved back to Puerto Rico while waiting for his license. There, he got introduced to pickleball. When he returned, we started drilling together, and I taught him everything he knows. Now he's the GM and head teaching pro at the Atlanta Pickleball Center, even competing in pro qualifiers. His life is very different because of pickleball," Wuerffel said.

Wuerffel also ties the sport to family.

"One of my favorite moments is when our family gets together for Christmas break. One time, we had my 79-year-old mom and dad playing alongside my brother and my eight-year-old nephew. In the summer, we do it again at my parents' house with all three generations. It's pretty crazy."

His passion has also blended with philanthropy.

"On December 13, the Wuerffel Foundation will again host the Pickle Bowl in New York during Heisman Trophy week. We'll have a bunch of Heisman guys paired with professionals. It's been a fun new way to fundraise," he said.

"Somebody even auctioned off a two-hour lesson with me at one of their events. I'm about to go do that, and it's been great."

Celebrities and athletes are also embracing the sport.

"Basketball gets harder as you age, but pickleball is something you can still enjoy. Even Tim Tebow loves it. At my event last year, Tebow and Cam Newton had one of the most epic points ever. Their celebration was incredible."

The growth extends to the college scene, with club teams and a national championship.

"I wouldn't be surprised if it becomes an official college sport before long. That would mean more training and scholarships, and eventually, high school pickleball becoming more than just a club activity," he said.

The only major challenge he sees is access to courts.

"In Florida, they have hundreds of kids in the club and not enough courts to play on."

Looking at the sport overall, Wuerffel sees lasting potential.

He says, "Pickleball is unique. It builds community, it's easy to start, and it keeps people active. Whether recreational or competitive, it's a game with a thousand levels. You can play it like checkers, or you can try to master it like chess."

Darius Christian

The Pickleball Tour

When the pandemic was in its final stages, Darius was effectively out of work.

He said, "I wasn't able to tour. I wasn't able to perform. A little bit of me was just going crazy."

He was used to a very active touring schedule most of the year, and was getting desperate for something to do.

"My family had a ping pong table in the basement, and I wanted to practice and play all the time. It wore my family out," he said.

During one of the games, his girlfriend at the time told Darius he should try pickleball.

"I was like, what is that? She didn't want to tell me because of what happened when I was introduced to ping pong."

The first time the ball hit the paddle, Darius had an "aha" moment.

"It was similar to the first time I started hearing music on the radio. The zoom focus showed up, things slowed down, and I felt a rewiring for the game."

Darius immediately jumped into the sport.

"I bought paddles, I bought balls, figured out which was best, and went on to the Playtime scheduler," he said.

Every time he visited a new city, there was an immediate search for nearby courts.

Darius said, "I would drive 45 minutes out to play with random people, and go back and play a show that night. And that's how my pickleball journey started."

What seemed like a simplistic move has helped Darius build his own global pickleball community.

"I can be anywhere in the world and find a game. Even in places like Melbourne, Australia, there's a community and great players. It's really fun building this hobby."

The first time Darius played pickleball, he was wearing jeans and boots.

He said, "I couldn't hit the ball really, but when contact was made it was like a chemical release."

Now, when he teaches people the game, Darius enjoys the process and the patience it takes.

As a lifelong learner, Darius continues to seek new knowledge.

"I got my master's in jazz studies, performance, and writing arrangement at NYU. And before that, I was teaching trombone lessons for middle school and high school kids," he said.

His lessons also included piano, bass, and guitar.

"The last couple of years, I transitioned to being a vocal coach as well. I had someone work with me for about six months so that she could sing at her wedding to her husband. So, I think my recreational play is very strong, very confident. I've played with

D1 tennis players and coaches or pro players at different facilities and have had great games," he said.

Darius knows he's still at the point where he needs to elevate his game with tournament experience to start medaling.

Giving insight to other players, Darius knows how important experience is.

"That's a big thing in music school. A lot of music education majors were there studying to teach. I was studying to perform," he said.

"I've now completed my teaching certification, and continue to play in high-level tournaments. It's an honor to instruct others in pickleball. I'm excited to continue to build this part of my life. Through my music, my passion for the game, and by sharing my story, I look forward to all that lies ahead," he said.

"You know, that's the game of learning. And I'm so addicted to that mental workout. You're always learning, whether it be a shot or a strategy. Flow state is definitely part of pickleball."

Darius compares this feeling to being on stage and curating the experience for the audience and the band.

"You have to stay present and aware of everything that's happening around you while you're aware of what you're doing."

He continues, "I find that when you're on the court in these high-pressure situations or entertaining folks at Necker Island or wherever, you are in the flow state."

Darius sees so many parallels between music and pickleball.

"There's so much improvisation happening with every point. If you are good, and if your partner's good, and are working well together, you're playing an amazing game."

Even on tour, Darius is thinking about pickleball.

"I have this obsessive thing in the morning where I wake up and I want to play. In Melbourne, I love hanging with some guys at this place called The Jar. But sometimes I just reach out at the last minute on a tour stop to find a game."

He continues, "Sometimes I'll do community events in the city with small groups of like 50 people. It would be pretty amazing to incorporate elements of entertainment and coaching in these sessions. Like on a show day, I could thank everyone for coming out and then invite them to the show that night. It's my vision to build community."

Darius loves how the game transcends geography.

He said, "It even transcends language. You can put two people on the other side of each other. They don't have to even talk. They can just go back and forth playing. It doesn't matter. So, I think the global community aspect of this sport is really fascinating."

Recently, Darius was invited to an event called the Necker Island Pickleball Forum, hosted by Richard Branson.

"It just felt so ridiculous that I questioned its validity until I was there. But upon my arrival, I think all of my questions were answered."

Now in its third year, the event attracted high-powered business executives, Hollywood personalities, professional athletes, and musicians.

Spending a few days with this unique group, Darius was truly moved.

"The second we all started playing pickleball, everyone knew why Richard brought us together. It was truly an experience to come together, to let our guard down, and just be present. I was so honored to attend, to share our vulnerability and enjoy the ridiculous beauty of his island."

He said, "Just yesterday, I found myself having a conversation while playing recreational pickleball here in Pasadena, California, with a group of men. The next thing I know, we're talking about ways that we can be more vulnerable in our partnerships and relationships. And I was like, 'Whoa, this is amazing. Four o'clock in the afternoon, just a group of guys talking about life.'"

Darius loves what the game is doing.

"Pickleball has become a safe space for people. I think it's just a calling to whatever this little plastic ball is doing for people."

He continues, "I'm not saying it was a gift from God, but it came at the perfect time after the pandemic with the chaos of the Universe. I mean, movement, togetherness, this is super cool, super important."

He said, "There is that mover and shaker energy where I feel a deeper connection happen at pickleball. I met this guy playing pickleball. He's like a 4.5 player in his 50's. We instantly connected."

Darius loves to throw intimate parties at his house and play acoustic music.

"My pickleball friends always show up with blankets and beer. They are always ready."

At a recent party, one of Darius's friends from the game showed up.

"His name is Dave. Great guy. We had been playing pickleball for about a year at that point. I realized that I had no idea what he did for work."

Darius found out that his friend was an animator at Paramount who had worked on films like *Shrek* and *Wild Robot*.

"You just never know who you will connect with in pickleball, and in life."

After being in Mumford & Sons for about a year, Darius had constantly tried to get band members to play.

"In past gigs, it was like pulling teeth to get anyone to play pickleball, but with these guys, everyone was interested."

He continues, "The next thing I know, we've got the horn section out on the court with the drummer, and I'm just giving out paddles. It was a beautiful thing!"

"The next thing I know, lead singer, Marcus, is out on the court with us in Sydney having a blast. And every time I see the crew between shows, they're like, 'hey man, did you pickle?' It's ridiculous and awesome," he said.

On a recent trip, Darius shared this story:

"I was just in Sydney and Billie Eilish was on tour, her team reached out to the Sydney Racquetball Club asking if Billie could show up and play. And they're like, sure mate, it's open. That being said, she showed up, and had a blast."

"One of the things that I'm running into is I'm so passionate, and my entrepreneurial ideas are always going. I want to be careful not to completely disrupt the whole magic of the game with monetization," he said.

"I get lots of paddles given to me to demo. But what I really enjoy is just giving them to my friends who are new to the sport."

Daryl Wyatt

Pickleball Down Under

When I interviewed Daryl, he had just completed a 20-hour flight from Australia to compete in the US Open in Naples.

He said, "Yesterday I competed in the Senior men's doubles and lost in the quarterfinals. Today I'll just practice and then play Senior pro men's on Wednesday."

"About a year and a half ago, I started playing. It happened after I bought a tennis club in Kansas City."

The club had lines for pickleball, but Daryl was a tennis player and resisted.

"I was one of those tennis guys who just didn't want to drink the juice. But when more and more members asked me to play, I realized it was the smartest business move."

Eventually, Daryl got out on the court for a game.

"I had a blast!"

It led him to start bringing in other pros to teach lessons to the member base.

He said, "One group, David George and Jen Gallwas, came in and were teaching a lesson and started telling me about the NPO. It's a national pickleball league for seniors."

"I really just wanted to start to play in the league. And so I asked them about it. They said how much of a great time they had."

This was the beginning of Daryl's professional journey into pickleball to try to qualify and play in the combine.

"I wanted to qualify or at least earn a spot to be drafted on one of the teams," he said.

There's no more tennis at the club.

"I had started out teaching eight hours a day on the court and let pickleball play on one of them."

Soon enough, the tennis scene eroded, and the courts were resurfaced.

"Now there's no tennis. It's all pickleball."

His club has 10 pickleball courts, with a second under construction.

"I also just opened a facility in Geelong, Australia in March, so I'm back and forth."

He said, "You know, I really hadn't followed pickleball or kept up with it prior to trying to play."

Now at 50, Daryl's life had been consumed by tennis.

"I played junior tennis, in college, and on the tour. My mind definitely wondered how much longer am I going to want to do this?"

Watching the landscape shift for both sports and losing his enthusiasm for tennis, Daryl decided it was time to make a change.

From the business side, Daryl has experienced much.

"It's been an unbelievable ride learning and profiting from the boom in the industry. It's been great and I'm very happy with the change."

He continues, "At 50, it's like a new lease on life. You are always learning something new."

Recently, playing at the US Open, Daryl was on TV as he competed on center court.

"Where else can you do that? It's just, it's remarkable what the sport is doing."

"Every day I tell people I can't believe what's happening in this industry."

"I hear some people complain, but where else can someone over 50 do something they enjoy, and make a little bit of money too? I laugh every day about it."

Daryl has seen pickleball fundamentally change his community.

"That's one of the things that really has influenced me and has made an impression upon me. Even at my club, I'll see people come who've never played a sport in their life, and they'll play a couple of times and develop new friendships," he said.

"With tennis, you can never go on as a coach and get some rallies or anything on with someone you're teaching. Whereas pickleball, I can go out and teach a lesson and still get something out of a lesson, get some play in, get some touches and feel like I'm actually having a good time, not just teaching and for the love of it, but actually learning from a player standpoint. It's amazing."

Like many who enjoy the game, Daryl loves the look on people's faces when they come off the court, even the first timers.

"I've rarely heard someone come off and say it was no fun. What I do hear consistently, whether you played just the first time or whether you play all the time, is that it was so much fun," he said.

"Coming from tennis and looking at the game from a player's perspective, I didn't realize I could get a workout on such a small court. I always thought it would be so easy. But every time I come, I look forward to playing again."

Daryl loves how the sport is for everybody.

"It doesn't matter what your skill level is, what your athletic level is. It's literally for everyone."

Back in Kansas City, Daryl marvels at how many tennis players have switched to pickleball.

"One day, an old tennis buddy comes to the club and I'm looking for his tennis bag. It's not there. I'm like, okay, maybe he's come with his friends. So I see him sitting at the table in the lobby and there's a pickleball paddle," he said.

"Just a few months ago we had both talked about how we will NEVER play pickleball. I guess that's all changed!"

Another time, Daryl was at an outdoor park, and he saw another tennis friend.

"He pulls up and he comes into park and before I'm on the first court, he rolls the window down and says, 'Hey, Daryl, I thought you'd never played pickleball outside either.'"

Watching his friend park, Daryl headed to the pickleball court.

"The next thing I know, he comes in with his pickleball bag, and he gets on the court next to me. I look at him and I say, 'Yeah, you drank the juice too.'"

Nowadays, Daryl sees other tennis alumni playing pickleball.

"I'll go play some tournaments and MLPs, and smirk at my friends about our new sport."

He continues, "I'm now part owner of the Kansas City Singers and also play for the team. This league's growing. It's for a senior 50 and over plus team. With all the teams sold, we ended up all going in and purchasing the local franchise and named it the Kansas City Stingers."

"The entire industry is kind of surprising me from several different standpoints. I've never seen anything grow like this in my life."

Daryl is in awe of the player side, the technology, and the money being thrown into the game.

"Just about everything has been a surprise to me, including opening a club in Australia," he said.

"Within our first month, we did a holiday camp and had almost 20 students attend. Now, mind you, pickleball is just starting to really take up over there, and we are still having this many kids come in."

With the camp being only one day, he immediately saw the impact.

"At the end of the first day, you'd see parents coming up to the desk and signing up for the rest of the week because their kids had so much fun."

When Daryl started converting his courts to pickleball, he wondered if it was just a fad.

"I decided to bank on the growth of the sport and made the right decision."

Every day since purchasing his club, Daryl has had new members sign up. Another thing that took him by surprise is how the members spend many hours at the club.

"It's interesting, because our members might play for two hours and stay for six. I'll have people come in, set up their laptops, eat, play games, and go back to work without ever leaving. It's insane."

One of the most promising things about the game that Daryl notices is that the junior side is really starting to pick up.

He said. "Pickleball used to be an old person's sport, and the youth didn't want to play. And I had one guy tell me just point blank that when he was 18 and started playing, he wouldn't tell his friends he was playing pickleball because they wouldn't understand why he liked the game."

Daryl has seen many junior players switch over to pickleball because of the ease of entry, the learning curve, and the ability to have fun.

"I've got kids who played tennis, and now they're coming back and only playing pickleball. Many have switched to pickleball because they got tired of just chasing tennis balls, because until you learn how to hit a tennis ball, you're just chasing and picking them up."

When he was still coaching tennis, Daryl shared this story.

"I had a young girl who worked so hard but just couldn't improve her game."

The only sport she played, his student was unable to sustain rallies, even though she loved being on the court.

He said, "One day I introduced her to pickleball. And on a recent trip to Australia, her mom shared a post on Instagram of this girl. She had just played her first pickleball tournament, medaled, and was so thankful for being introduced to the sport."

Daryl has seen many juniors transform.

"I see their confidence grow, and how much they enjoy playing the game. For me, that's what it's all about."

Even with adults, the game is making a profound impact.

"I had one lady come to the club, pulling me aside to share her experiences with the game," he said.

"You can tell how athletically challenged she is, even seeing her stumble when simply walking sometimes. A powerful local business executive, she was so happy to share with me how the game has changed her life in ways she would never imagine."

For Daryl, choosing this path in his own life continues to have its rewards.

"Pickleball has given me a whole new group of friends and a community. I didn't know any of these people before I started playing pickleball, but these are my friends now."

Devin Alexander
The Pickleball Chef

The very first time Devin saw pickleball was as a member at Manhattan Country Club in Manhattan Beach.

"They started taking away our tennis courts for pickleball courts and people were up in arms."

She received a call one day from a friend in a panic.

"My friend asked me to sub in for a mini tournament. I had no idea what I was doing or how to score and messed up so many times."

Devin and her partner ended up having a good showing, as she was in the entry-level group.

"It was kind of fun. But then again, I didn't want to do this as opposed to tennis."

It wasn't until moving to a new community with a pickleball court that she gave it another chance.

"I was one of those tennis people who was never going to leave the sport. But then I realized the mass number of people playing and the fact that I needed to make friends in a new community, and it seemed like the best way to do it."

Moving from California to Pennsylvania, Devin was seeking a way to work out. Tennis was not readily accessible to her as a single mom.

"I was finding myself not being as fit as I like and not finding options to work out without spending like a hundred dollars every time I wanted to go play tennis for childcare, or busting up all of my workdays."

So, she had a radical idea. On a snowy weekend during Martin Luther King Day, Devin decided to create a pickleball court.

"In addition to not having school on Monday, we ended up not having school two other days that week. So, we played every single day because we had plenty of time with the kids at home," he said.

"I went and ordered a pickleball net and built a court in my basement. Because I had so much space, it was almost a regulation court."

Soon, Devin's daughter and friends started playing on one side, with the moms on the other.

"I got super addicted to it. And then when spring rolled around, I jumped into it in the community where I lived," he said.

"The kids sometimes played with us, but more often it was just half of my basement court with the kids on the other half."

Devin got the idea to paint the basement.

"I made it look like the deck of a Royal Caribbean ship in beautiful turquoise. It brightened up the space so much."

The fun continued, with the girls spray-painting furniture for the kids' area.

"We even brought down chairs and games and made it a fun place to hang out."

Devin's girlfriend and she started to play almost every day.

"She loved my advice on losing weight, and our daughters were becoming best friends."

Some days, Devin even caught herself hitting the ball against the wall.

"We came up with a game called "Thirties," where we would try to do thirty hits back and forth on purpose with little dinks and things. It helped me to pick up my game quickly when I went outside."

That winter, Devin moved again.

"I wanted to get my daughter into a better school. But the community was basically a vacation town."

Luckily, Devin found plenty of pickleball at the local rec center.

"They had games three days a week in the winter. I would literally work, play pickleball, and go on a few dates. The town was mostly older people, but it became like my retreat."

When the warmer weather finally came, the games moved outdoors.

"People come from all the local towns to play here. This last July 4th, we had over 150 people playing in a two-hour block of time. It was ridiculous, there were paddles lined up for days."

"Pickleball has built my entire social footprint on the East Coast of the United States. I play whenever I can and always socialize," he said.

"It's a great workout if you do it right. I know it looks like it would be, but no matter who you are playing with, there are plenty of athletic movements. And I just love how social it is. People always seem to be in a good mood around pickleball."

With exercise an important component of her life, Devin always thought she hated working out.

"I went to a Biggest Loser resort and was being paid to take three-hour hikes every day. And I was like, my God, this is heaven."

She soon realized that she had always thought working out was a waste of time.

"With pickleball, I've loved it because it's a thought process also. I like the strategy in it and it makes two hours go by in no time flat instead of rotting on a treadmill where I'd be like, 'Oh my God, get me off this thing,'" he said.

"One of the things that I love about pickleball is that anybody can pick up a paddle and kind of do it. I've actually been helping a little seven-year-old that I met at the rec center. She and her family were there, and they didn't really know how to play," he said.

"My daughter hit it off with one of their other daughters, who also didn't want to play. So, I just stayed to help the seven-year-old who did like to play and her family. It was amazing to watch how quickly this little girl got so good, because she wanted to."

Devin loves how easy the game can be.

"You can always practice your dinks and other parts of the game with anybody who can sort of hit it back, if that makes sense."

She has seen many people resist the game until their friends get into it.

"It's easy to have conversations and to be fun and funny."

At her home court, Devin always looks forward to summer play.

"We have 14 courts at our facility. When the whistle blows, you go to play your game. If you win, you stay. If you lose, you go off and stack your paddles. After two games, everyone comes off."

Devin loves the flexibility of the game.

"It doesn't matter if you come late or not. And for me as a single mom, it was really nice."

She compares the game to on-demand exercising and socializing.

"I would love for my work to overlap into pickleball."

Her cookbooks (https://devinalexander.com/books/) are all focused on healthy eating.

"If I wrote another one, it would probably be more of a pickle potluck or something like that."

Devin thinks there needs to be more pickleball clothes for women.

"I've been doing some work with QVC and want to figure out how to bring more options to the market."

Dustin and Lisa DeMeritt

Pickles and Dinky Balls

In June 2020, Lisa was invited to play pickleball.
"I was an athlete growing up and was always working out. As soon as I tried the game, I was hooked and became addicted."

That night, she went home and told Dustin that she was pretty good.

"It reignited my competitive fire, as I knew I could do this and own it."

Later that year, Dustin returned to visit family in Kansas and told them about Lisa's addiction to pickleball.

"They immediately told me about Chicken N Pickle," says Dustin. "When I got home and told my wife, she loved the idea and thought we should do something similar here in Massachusetts, minus the chicken."

"We were perfectly positioned to make this happen," says Lisa. "With my passion for the game, and Dustin's expertise in building a brand, we decided to launch Pickles."

So, the couple went to work brainstorming in the middle of COVID.

Looking for space to put the club, local landlords had no idea what Dustin and Lisa were talking about.

"While sitting in front of them, they would be on their phones googling what pickleball was. They had some confidence in our business plan but also asked what it would take to convert the space back to its original condition."

Dustin continues, "We were thinking of a business launch, and they were thinking of an exit strategy."

"We had no idea how to start a business, and we weren't even particularly good pickleball players."

Lisa continues, "All we knew is that we didn't want to be in the entertainment or the food business. We wanted to be in the pickleball business."

At the time, it seemed like a crazy idea.

"How are you going to make enough money to be profitable when people don't think they have to pay to play pickleball because outside courts are free," says Dustin. "There were no models to draw from and tremendous risk."

Lisa and Dustin scoured the country looking for another pickleball club.

"All we found locally was a sports facility that put nets out on basketball courts a few days a week."

She continues, "All I found elsewhere was a place in Virginia called Pickleballerz that had just opened. The owner and I spoke often, and she gave us the confidence to do this ourselves."

Getting a liquor license in Massachusetts during COVID was nearly impossible.

"You couldn't be a bar, and had to serve hot food," says Dustin.

After spending an additional $30,000 to put in commercial sinks and a kitchen grease trap, the couple found out that they could buy a twenty-dollar hot dog machine, put it on the counter, and secure the license.

"So, we got our license, and opened the club," says Lisa.

To this day, neither the grease trap nor the hot dog machine has been used and both remain as an ode to what was needed to secure the liquor license.

"It's what inspired our slogan, 'Where Pickleball Fanatics Gather to Dink and Drink'."

The court reservation system was a whole other challenge.

"We searched for something to use and found a platform that a beauty salon used to manage their tanning bed reservations online," says Dustin. "So, when Pickles opened, you were effectively booking a tanning bed as a court to play pickleball. And owners think TODAY is the 'Wild West.' We have come a long way since 2021."

That risk turned into their ultimate success, with Pickles opening in March of 2021.

"We saw explosive growth," says Lisa. "It gave people a place to go and be themselves, let loose, and not have any restrictions on themselves playing outside. Even inside, we still had to wear masks."

"At Pickles, you play pickleball. That's it."

Lisa continues, "When a lot of us played in the afternoon, what we really wanted after was a beer. So, our slogan was 'Where pickleball fanatics gather to dink and drink.' Here, our goal is to get people to linger longer."

"We always had a 3-5-year plan to exit the business," says Dustin. "Even as it was getting launched, we were fielding offers from interested buyers. It was then that we knew we had something special."

"Every day, I was on the phone coaching others how to build their own facility."

Lisa continues, "We even had a discussion with Jorge Barragan of Picklr about franchising. Guess they beat us to the punch!"

Pickles turned into a family atmosphere quickly.

"A lot of people lost their friend base during COVID, and our club helped them build it back up," says Lisa. "Little by little, we saw new social groups form where they would do things together after pickleball."

"One of our most successful innovations was creating something called the 'Pickle Play Lab'," says Dustin. "We invited twenty-four new people to experience the game with a free lesson. Our format was fifteen-minute intervals where we taught the history of the game, simple hitting, how to score, and then playing a game."

Their model was a huge success.

"Most coming through the door had never played. But after, many would buy a paddle, sign up for a lesson, or join the club."

Lisa continues, "We started signing up groups of twenty-four, and the club exploded. Our story became so widely known that we were featured in the first edition of Pickleball Magazine."

"One of my favorite stories is about a member named Marguerite," says Lisa. "She's a flight attendant, a widow, in her 70s, and had a support dog called 'Mr. Jefferson.' Marguerite walked in the club, never having played pickleball before."

She continues, "To this day, she still works for the airline and plays pickleball as much as possible. She'll tell you that pickleball changed her life, and that Pickles and its members became her new family."

Three and a half years later, the couple decided to sell Pickles.

"It seemed like the right time, as the business was booming and the sport was continuing to grow," says Dustin. "It was definitely a seller's market with so many pickleball enthusiasts trying to break into the business. We priced Pickles aggressively, received tremendous interest, and had it sold just a few months later."

"So, the story doesn't end," says Lisa. "Our next adventure was actually brewing for some time. It's called Dinky Balls."

Hatched at the family dinner table, Dustin and Lisa would tell their kids stories from work.

"We came up with names for our members (Banger, Lobber, Whacko, etc.) and started toying around with the idea of creating a collection of these pickleball player personalities."

At Pickles, the staff and coaches also started labeling all of the members.

"We just had fun with it to start, as we always thought of our club as the land of misfit toys," says Lisa. "The stories became the foundation of our twelve characters and badges of honor where you own who you are, play your own style of pickleball, and just 'be you'."

Lisa is now out on the courts, always playing.

"I'll let someone know which Dinky Balls personality they play like and give them a sticker with the character."

The couple knows the only way to scale is with brand awareness, and they prefer the small environment of pickleball courts by building brand awareness one player at a time.

"So, we visit the island of St. John's often," says Dustin. "On one trip, we decided to put a Pickles sticker inside an open taxi. On our next visit, we were in the same taxi and placed a Dinky Balls sticker next to it."

He continues, "A few months ago, we saw a social media post where a pickleball player took a picture of the stickers in the taxi and shared it. How cool is that?"

Dustin and Lisa know how important the game is to our youth.

"It's important to share pickleball with the kids, and Dinky Balls is one more way to do that."

He continues, "We love seeing kids get off their phones and play pickleball with their friends and families. That's generational magic."

"Our journey now with Dinky Balls is to find ways to keep making positive impacts in the community," says Lisa. "The game matters, it makes a difference, and gives something to everyone who plays it. One day, we want our children to tell their kids how pickleball became part of our country's fabric and how Dinky Balls played a small part in that."

Emily Akradi

A Lifetime of Pickleball

"While bringing my kids to tennis lessons, our instructor, Mo Alhouni (now a pro pickleball player), kept trying to get me to take some lessons. He eventually gave up on that idea and asked if I had heard of pickleball. I had no idea what it was."

Emily went on YouTube to watch some videos on the game. "I decided to go pick up some paddles, tape off a tennis court and give it a try."

She continues, "It turned out that some of the Lifetimes had pickleball leagues where they played on the basketball courts. Obviously, it wasn't that big because I never even heard of it."

"It was love at first sight. This game is so much fun, so great. And you're active. You don't even realize you're active because you're having so much fun."

Soon, Emily started inviting more and more people to play with her. Once getting the hang of the game, she approached Bahram, the CEO of Lifetime.

"He totally shot me down and had no idea what pickleball was."

She persisted and was directed to the Head of Tennis.

"I kept bugging them both and finally got through to Bram to at least try it," she said.

"It wasn't easy, as Bahram was a hardcore tennis player who thought that pickleball would ruin his game."

Emily continues, "Literally, he loved it. I don't think he's played tennis since, so it has ruined his tennis game."

Bahram quickly found out about the game being played on basketball courts, and the chaos it was causing. So, he took a tennis court in Eden Prairie and turned it into three pickleball courts. Instantly, the courts were jam-packed.

Says Emily, "There's a lot of people with great ideas, but he's the guy that can make it happen."

From that point forward, Lifetime went on a full court press, rolling out pickleball courts nationwide.

"I think there's close to 800 courts now at Lifetime Pickleball, and there's still a crazy amount of demand. It's been super fun. I love it."

A big part of Lifetime's business now is these healthy living complexes where you have the apartment buildings, the gym, the pool, the cafe, and your workspace. There's no reason to leave.

Says Emily, "It's driven our revenue through the roof. I don't know specific numbers, but I know it's all because of pickleball. Lifetime is now dominating the pickleball scene, and no one's going to come close to it. I'm still waiting for my cut."

"I've made a lot of new friends with pickleball, which is great. I'm still working on my oldest friends to try to get them to play, but now they're saying I'm too good for them. But I'll play with anyone, it's all good."

Emily takes the game in stride.

"I bought my original paddle at Dick's Sporting Goods. Don't see how a $300 paddle is going to make me a better player."

She sees the trend towards players wanting the latest and greatest, thinking it will improve their games.

"You do need to have the right shoes to play."

Says Emily, "Everyone's jumping on the pickleball craze with not only the paddles, but also with the tennis shoes, and skirts. Is a pickleball skirt any different than a tennis skirt? But if you call it pickleball, then you get a whole different group that wants the pickleball outfits."

"Unfortunately, we are seeing lots of injuries from this craze."

Emily knows that overplay is the cause.

"They're doing pickleball two hours a day, every day, seven days a week. And then they're not adding in the muscle training and the stretching and the rest of the stuff that helps prevent injuries," she said.

"So, I just came from a women's pickleball travel league that we have in Minnesota. I'm playing for our St. Louis Park location. One week there will be drills, the next week we will have a match between the clubs."

Emily loves the game so much.

"I used to do a lot of mountain bike racing in the past, and some triathlons. But I got to a point where I just don't like cardio. It's just so boring. So, pickleball, I'm getting that great lower-level cardio without even realizing that I'm getting it in. It's been so fun."

Like many, Emily is following the game on social media.

"I'm just doing Instagram. I love the pro's feeds where they will post drills, tips and even tournament results. They have lots of good advice," she said.

"Pickleball is a fun social way of being active that any age group can play. I can't go on a tennis court and pick up a tennis match and have fun with that. I'm too competitive for that. But with pickleball, I can play with my son (who's now a varsity tennis player), my daughters (10 and 12), and even my mom."

Emily knows that when someone starts the game, they can be nervous and timid.

She said, "Six months later, they're transformed and feel like a new person. I love that. I love the confidence it's giving people, not only in just doing something but getting better at it and seeing the improvement. That's the great thing about pickleball. You really can see improvement, month after month. So, it's good."

Emily continues, "You do see different personalities for sure. I hope to always be fun, easygoing, easy to play with, good attitude, and good sportsmanship."

Emily likes to make everyone feel comfortable.

"You're always going to see people at different levels and don't want to make them feel bad. I don't target the weaker player when we play mixed doubles or doubles. I also like playing with people who are way better than me, because it just makes me better. And I don't mind being the weak link of the four."

Playing since the pandemic ended, Emily has thought about building a court on her farm.

"We've got a grass tennis court that my kids play on. We've thought about it and just haven't done it. And so, we just drive to the courts because there are so many nearby."

"It's so cool," says Emily. "I mean, there are a few things in life where you really can't have your phone glued to your hips. But pickleball is one of them. It's awesome. If you can find things to do every day that take you away from your phone, that's winning."

Erica Desai and Mary Cannon

CityPickle

Erica and Mary met through their children. "We both have daughters who just last week graduated high school, and we met when they were two and in nursery school."

Over the years, they spent lots of time together, including on the tennis court.

Says Mary, "I think one of the things that's been most meaningful for me, is that both Erica and I left pretty hard-charging careers to be stay-at-home parents."

During that time, Mary leaned into the nonprofit world.

"I served as national board chairs for nonprofits, but we weren't being paid for our work."

It was a theme that continued.

Erica first learned to play pickleball in 2021.

"It was during COVID, and I went on a trip with my husband and another couple to a resort in Vermont. And they taught us how to play pickleball at an intro clinic. It was so much fun!"

Coming back to New York, she wanted to play more but found that nearly impossible as there were few courts built.

"In a city known for being a leader, and one that I lived in for the last 30 years, it was way behind in pickleball," she said.

"I actually had a very similar experience to Erica. I was on a couple's trip in South Carolina and played pickleball for the first time," says Mary.

"I thought I was going on a tennis trip because both Erica and I love tennis. And instead, we played pickleball. I think one of the things that really captured me was that I played with a beer in my hand, and I thought that that was pretty fun. Pretty great way to socialize."

With the lack of courts, players resorted to chalking cracked asphalt spaces with lines and setting up their own nets.

"At the time," says Erica, "there were no dedicated pickleball courts in New York City. Nowhere where you could make a reservation and play according to your own schedule."

Focused on real estate and finance at the time, Mary was working with a business partner to find a space to open a youth sports program in the city.

"My partner Eve and I had both played college sports and raised athletic kids in the city."

With such a shortage of youth sports activities and even less space to create something, the challenge was great.

When COVID hit, Erica and Mary started thinking more about pickleball.

She said, "It was more of a light bulb for Erica because I can remember so specifically in August of '21 saying, 'You know how you and Eve have that thing that you're working on? What if we made it pickleball instead? And then we were off to the races.'"

"I actually have a pickleball court at my home in Bucks County, Pennsylvania," says Mary.

Both her and Erica got in lots of pickleball, until they decided to go into business together. With three teenagers, the court is used often.

"Now I lose to them regularly, as most are in college. It's a little disappointing."

From that moment on, Erica and Mary went all in on the idea.

"Eve had to step away to focus on her four children."

City Pickle was created to bring the sport of pickleball to dense urban areas.

"In cities like New York, the barrier to entry is high and so is the demand," says Mary.

Both think that soon, suburban areas will be oversupplied.

She said, "Accessibility is a wonderful thing and is going to fuel the sport."

"We chose the name City Pickle very intentionally," says Erica.

"From the beginning, our goal was to be in cities across the country. That's why we started where we live. Because you know they say, 'If you can make it here, you can make it anywhere.' And we are living proof of that."

For Erica and Mary, a big part of their model is around events.

"It's been our experience that pickleball events are very appealing for all kinds of situations, but especially for corporate events because they are excellent for team building and clients," says Mary.

They know that each location is close to many corporate headquarters, which helps drive the business model.

"We have multiple clubs and activations in New York City and Philadelphia, and will soon break ground in Boca Raton," Erica says.

The business has expanded in partnerships with companies like Related and is also focusing on merchandise sales.

"We're super proud of our online retail store that we recently launched. It provides a great supplementary stream of revenue."

City Pickle is primarily a brand that operates courts.

Says Mary, "It's really the real estate. Our main model is long-term leases. We are doing the Long Island City Club and Times Square as examples."

Each indoor facility is climate-controlled where brand awareness and activations can help drive the pickleball business.

"So many people still haven't played, and everybody's heard about it at this point, but many people have not put a paddle in their hand yet."

"During the pandemic, our goal was to create a place where people could come together in real time and in real space and share experiences with each other because it was just so desperately needed at that time," Erica says.

"And it continues to be extremely important."

Both Erica and Mary know that building a community is behind all of the things they do when making business decisions.

Right from the beginning, City Pickle was created from scratch.

"We are very mindful about our brand voice. And we talk a lot about wanting to convey fun, wanting you to feel like your best self when you're at a City Pickle location," says Mary.

"We sort of do the nod to Cheers, that place where everybody knows your name and you want to go back again and again."

In an industry dominated by men, Erica and Mary are proud to be a woman-founded and women-led business.

Says Erica, "We actually think that that's been a little bit of our spidey superpower. Whether it's an intense eye for detail and organization, brand voice our graphics, we make sure that women are well represented in the sport from players on the courts through senior leadership."

"I do think it is very appealing to be a part of a sport that is equally played by men and women. And I don't think that's typical, or I can't think of another sport where that's the case," says Mary.

"I love the egalitarian nature of that. So, when businesses want to get together, I think this is what I love about corporate events."

"City Pickle has really leaned into youth programming. We have after-school classes all semester long. We have summer camp. We do a lot of kids' and teen birthday parties. As parents ourselves, we know what is important for these offerings."

They also partner with many non-profits.

Says Erica, "We provide free court programming and time with coaches to groups like The Boys Club and Harlem Ice Hockey. The pickleball industry has not reached out enough to under-resourced communities yet. We are going to change that."

"We think pickleball solves everything," says Mary.

"We've never seen anybody leave the pickleball court and not have a smile on their face. Right. And that's kind of the special sauce of pickleball. You know, it spreads that joy."

Erica and Mary are committed to welcoming everyone to the game. With pickleball, it's about trying new things.

"We want to maintain that ethos so that people can come in and easily try the sport and become part of what's happening. They don't have to feel like they missed their window to be a part of the sport."

Both are very cognizant that that is still the largest group of people that are out there.

"Anybody is welcome to play at all of our locations. You need not be a member," says Erica.

"That's something that we will never change because we are always building our community. One of the things we are most proud of is hosting Queer Pickle every Friday night."

She continues, "It's super popular and sells out every time. The more court space we add, the more people who come."

Erica and Mary know that pickleball is the perfect vehicle for them.

"People are social, they stay for drinks afterwards and love the community feel."

Says Mary, "It's a community that started in a pretty organic way that we have supported. And now it's like a pillar of our weekend programming."

Ernie and Loida Medina

Pickleball for Life

In January of 2016, Ernie was attending a health fair at a college in Canada.

"I saw a demonstration of pickleball then, but it was in passing and I didn't give it another thought."

But a few months later in Michigan, his mother (Loida) brought him to her gym at church.

"Mom had been introduced to the game by a friend and shared it with me. That's when I really got to hit the ball."

The two fell in love with the game immediately.

Says Loida, "I came from tennis, which is harder to master. But pickleball is so much easier to learn and so enjoyable. That's why I still do it."

Returning from Michigan to Loma Linda, Ernie was unable to find any pickleball games.

"I looked in a 60-mile radius. Nothing. There were games in Palm Springs, L.A., and Pasadena. But the valley was quiet."

Buying a net, Ernie and Loida started playing in the driveway.

Ernie said, "When I returned from Michigan, we got a group, which we called the 'OG Nine', and started playing at a public tennis court," says Ernie.

"That was the summer of 2016. From then, the game just exploded all around Loma Linda."

"Over the next few years, our founding group got pickleball started in cities all through the valley," says Ernie.

"It's been great to see the groups formed, the clubs started, and the addition of so many new courts."

"As an Assistant Professor of Health at Loma Linda University, part of my job is to work with lifestyle-related diseases, whether it's diabetes, obesity, hypertension, heart disease, or cancer," says Ernie.

"And one of the root causes is your physical activity, or lack thereof."

Throughout his career, Ernie has remained active and inspires others to do the same.

"I was into mountain biking, ultimate frisbee, sports like that. But most of my patients are older, diabetic, overweight and can't do that type of activity. Then pickleball came along and I was like a light bulb went off. I was like, wow!"

Ernie loves how welcoming pickleball is.

"I can't just walk up to an ultimate frisbee game and hop in. But with pickleball, it's the opposite."

The experiment has proven itself, as Ernie has shown up unannounced at courts in Canada, Japan, and even the Philippines.

"Every time, I've been invited on the court to play. It's been great."

"Here was a sport that could overcome all the excuses on why a patient wouldn't exercise," says Ernie.

He would always hear things like: It's too expensive, I don't have enough time, it's not fun, I don't have access to it, it's too intense, it's too difficult.

"Pickleball just seemed to answer all those questions."

Ernie loves how scalable the game is.

"I can play with my mom. She can play with her grandkids. And we can have a great time."

He also appreciates the flexibility.

Says Ernie, "I could also be playing at a very high, intense level. And then the next game, I could be playing with first timers. I can't think of any other sport that I could do that with."

"I've played in cul-de-sacs, I've played in driveways, I've played in parking lots, I've played in hotel lobbies, I've played in airport hangars," Ernie said.

"I've played literally wherever we could set up that net. And I do this thing called 'exercise evangelism'. As a Christian, I go to churches, and I will do a talk on how to use friendship or exercise evangelism to bring people to their church and develop friendships."

Ernie has brought pickleball into the equation.

"At these small churches in L.A., I've set up pickleball courts in their parking lot to show them how they can do something to invite people over to their place and make friends that way."

He continues, "I've seen lots of churches, at least here in the area, using pickleball now as an outreach tool, as a way to reach the community."

While on a visit to a big church in Riverside, Ernie got introduced to the senior pastor.

"When I introduced myself, he said he had been looking forward to meeting the pickleball guru."

He continues, "It turns out he plays pickleball with his pastors. So now we're trying to get this what I'm calling 'Pastors and Parishioners Pickleball Palooza'."

"For me, I look at pickleball probably a little differently than most people. It's not just a fun sport. It's like a public health intervention that I think should be used anywhere and everywhere," Ernie said.

"One of my doctoral students is researching pickleball and the social connectedness in relation to decreasing isolation."

Ernie loves how his mom has embraced the game.

"She does it regularly with a wide range of people from young kids to university students, all the way up to adults and seniors. She and I have met so many people through pickleball that we otherwise would never have met."

A well-known personality in Loma Linda is always at the courts watching games.

"He calls himself the judge," says Loida.

"If there were any arguments about line calls, they would turn to him, and he'd yell out something and then start laughing because he couldn't really see what had just happened."

"I've used pickleball in my diabetes class," says Ernie.

"These are people that are overweight and out of shape, and that's partly why they're diabetic."

Getting them out on court, he gets each to just start dinking.

"I watch them getting red in the face, they're sweating, they're huffing and puffing from dinking. But yet the one thing that I always notice is that they're all smiling, they're all laughing, they're all having a good time."

Retiring from a long career as a physician, Loida now enjoys life to its fullest.

"I retired in 2023, at the ripe young age of 84," says Loida.

Not a traditional snowbird, Loida travels all over.

"We just got back from a trip to the Philippines and Japan this past summer."

On a recent visit to California, the two finally played in their first tournament together.

"Mom has always wanted me to play with her, so we played in the 60+ senior day, and I went down a skill level."

Ernie continues, "They let me play with her in 3.0, but I had to play left-handed. It was all ages, and we were the oldest combined team."

It was soon after that Loida went in for cataract surgery.

"If God did not give me this game, I would not be as active as I am now. I owe it all to pickleball," says Loida.

"I play twice a day, three times a week. The mornings are for the young players, and at night I play with my Phillipinos."

In between, Loida goes to the wellness center.

"I love sharing the energy, getting loud during points, and having fun. At the end of the day, being tired is good."

Loida enjoys playing with all of her family.

"I have three grandsons and one granddaughter, and play with them all. I want to play till 100."

It's been a busy few years for the "Godmother of Pickleball."

Says Loida, "I got that title after playing an exhibition game with the pros."

And rounding out her journey, Loida was featured in a Netflix series called *Live to 100: Secrets of the Blue Zone - Loma Linda*.

Ernie has seen pickleball open many doors.

"I got invited to a special lunch because the president of the Republic of Palau Micronesia was here and in conversations with the dean of the School of Business at LaSiera University, pickleball came up."

Says Ernie, "So then the president told my dean that the two of us had gone to college together. And I was told that pickleball is growing on the island of Palau, so I can't wait to go there someday to play."

"I love pickleball because it's totally changed all aspects of my life," says Ernie, "from my physical activity side, from my social side, from my work side. Now, here at the university, I'm not known as Dr. Medina. Everybody from the president on down knows me as the pickleball guy or the pickleball professor."

Evan Slaughter

For the Fun of the Game

Fighting an addiction to opiates, Evan first heard of pickleball while in rehab, after serving in the military from 2010–2014. Part of his tour was in Afghanistan.

"My ankle was messed up pretty bad, but I didn't want to leave deployment. So, I turned down the option to leave and have surgery and finished my 12-month deployment," He said.

The recovery eventually happened, but being on pain medications led to addiction issues.

"I had struggled on and off when I got out of the military in 2014 with getting sober, as there was an addiction issue in my family even before I served. Then, in 2021, I went back to the treatment center for a three-month program. It's one of the best things I've done in my life."

When Evan arrived, some of the guys kept telling him about pickleball.

"You gotta play pickleball with us. You're gonna love it."

Growing up playing racquetball, Evan was familiar with paddle sports.

He continues, "So I started playing it and fell in love with pickleball."

The facility was located in Alabama and run by a non-profit.

Says Evan, "It was beautiful, sitting on several acres of land out in the rural country. The pickleball court was a half basketball court made out of concrete, and the net was droopy and saggy."

Not the official length of a court, the players had to make modifications.

"We would put a piece of plywood down and stand on it to serve from for it to be long enough to be an official pickleball court," Said.

"The equipment wasn't great, but the point of it was that it was really, really fun. The guys that are there playing it, you know, we are all going through crap just from coming off drugs and alcohol,To be able to laugh again was huge. I love laughing and believe it's a form of medicine."

After Evan left rehab, he found a court to play on.

"Only then did I realize how big and popular it was becoming."

Right around the same time, Evan started doing social media content for a living.

"It's been the best job I've ever had. It's the first job where it doesn't feel like one, and I feel like I'm carrying out my purpose."

He continues, "I love bringing laughter and humor to people's lives and sharing my story once I do that. So, I started making some funny pickleball videos and posting them."

"Honestly, I was just doing it for fun and just to try to make some comedy videos."

Soon, Evan's videos started gaining traction and took off, leading him to become a pickleball influencer.

"Now I've got a five-year deal with a pickleball paddle company and my own paddle with my face on it. I've been hit up by just about anyone and everyone. If it pertains to marketing something in the pickleball space, they contact me."

With a following of nearly 300k on Instagram and a similar audience on TikTok, Evan has amassed a large audience.

"I think I have one of the most viral pickleball videos out there with almost 13 million views on Instagram and TikTok. Yeah, it's been crazy," he said.

"I live in Nashville now and go back every now and then to visit the rehab center. I talk with the director of the place all the time and donate 10% of my income directly to the facility."

Evan got Valer to donate 50 paddles.

He continues, "I actually have plans to build them a new court. And I am trying to figure out the best way to do it by raising money."

Entering the social media world, Evan left out that he was a veteran.

"People started noticing things like I wear this memorial bracelet and would ask why."

When Evan was injured, another soldier died. The bracelet is a tribute.

"I've kind of leaned down that avenue a little bit more as I've gone along. I've got a deal with the American Legion and make content to help promote them," he said.

"I just signed a deal with a company that does energy drinks. They're a veteran-owned company that's putting them in all the military bases because energy drinks are huge in the military community."

Evan is slowly seeing more efforts to bring the game of pickleball to the vertical.

Now an avid player, Evan has regular games with a group of friends.

"Now I'm showing my friends how to play and give them paddles and free gear that I'm getting all the time."

He continues, "I was debating whether to live in Austin or Nashville. It's huge in Texas, with lots of places to play. But it's just not like that in Nashville."

With friends and family near Nashville, he decided to stay.

Says Evan, "It's just because it's closer to my family and where I'm from."

One of his clients wanted to build him a pickleball court. Living in an apartment downtown, it wasn't going to happen.

"Ironically, my brother has nine acres nearby and was building a big barn. I asked if he wanted a pickleball court built next to it, and we made it happen," Evan said.

Now Evan films content there and has friends over to play.

"It's been really, really cool."

Evan travels extensively now.

"I've been to most tournaments and on TV. We have many projects under development, and I'm sure some will actually happen."

He's even done commentating for some matches.

"I think if I could get up every morning and do one thing in pickleball, it would just be a doubles match. I would play a morning doubles match at my pickleball court with a group of friends, and just some fun doubles in the evening."

One of Evan's favorite influencers is also a veteran. His name is Zachary Bell.

"He's got an account called 'Veteran with a Sign' where he literally stands in different places holding up a big piece of cardboard with some kind of statement on it. It's usually around military related stuff."

Living in Nashville, Evan reached out.

"He had never played before, so we got together and made some content around it. I gave him some paddles, and he's grown to love the sport."

Evan says, "I get messages all the time from veterans where they just talk about how I've helped them and what pickleball did for them. For me, it's mental health, it's physical health, socialization, getting out, not being isolated. And a lot of veterans that were in combat or injured in combat struggle with that."

"It's starting to become something that you see more in rehabs."

Evan continues to get messages about his efforts.

"I do some merch stuff and sell it online. It's usually around something funny I've said in a video. One of them says 'I learned pickleball in rehab.' People message me all the time about this."

Evan's efforts continue to have a profound effect.

"I get asked all the time from other treatment facilities that want pickleball there, and how to do it."

Now the Nashville market is expanding.

Says Evan, "There are some public places to play. The company that built my courts is working on a big indoor facility for Pickleball Kingdom. It's really helped the community here."

He continues, "I'm always trying to do something new or grow in an area."

With a new lease on life, Evan has much going on.

"I'm starting to do more stuff on YouTube in long-form content. I also have an idea for a show."

Stand-up comedy is another dream of Evan's.

"I also work with a clothing company called Chubbies and have been with them for a few years."

He continues, "They're doing a show called *Firsts with Evan*, where it's basically me going around doing things for the first time. And they had me do standup comedy on one of the episodes for the first time here at Zanies in Nashville. And I loved it."

Geoff Nyugen

The Courts at Piccadilly

"Before COVID started, I had just learned how to play the game through a friend of mine. We had been talking about playing tennis together because we both used to play it back in high school. It was his stepmom who introduced him to the game of pickleball," says Geoff.

Like most, he fell in love with the sport the moment he played it.

When all the parks closed, Geoff decided to rent a property in Tarzana that had a tennis court.

"I just taped pickleball lines, bought a temporary net, and some friends and I would go out there every weekend and play."

At the time, his good friend was also taking lessons from a senior pro named Scott Crandall.

With no other places to play, Scott asked Geoff if he could come to the house and practice. He was coaching a professional pickleball player named Jessie Irvine.

"Having set up two courts, Geoff immediately agreed. The pros would play on one court, and we were on the other. Two others who came were Gabe Joseph and Jeff Warnick. That was my introduction to professional pickleball," he said.

"We had such a blast at our private courts that I decided to buy this property out in Arcadia."

There, Geoff built what came to be known as The Courts at Piccadilly.

"I built four courts in my backyard on an oversized tennis court just so there's enough running space and everything. It became this hotspot for some of the top players in Los Angeles."

A few months after his purchase, Major League Pickleball was starting up.

"It was set up to compete directly against the PPA as a team format model."

His good friend Mark introduced him to Richie Tuazon, who had already bought the California Black Bears.

"He told me a little bit about how they were planning an expansion, and they were going to sell some teams. And I told him I was interested," he said.

"At that time, I think the expansion teams were being priced out at a million dollars each. So, I put my name in the hat, and I asked if it's possible for me to buy one of them and be a part of Major League Pickleball."

Seeing the growth of professional pickleball, Geoff knew it was an opportunity he didn't want to miss.

At the time, Geoff was noticing the league wanted more influential owners.

"That's why you saw names like LeBron James, Naomi Osaka, and other big names buying into these teams. And so I wasn't able to get in. They wouldn't sell a team to me," Geoff said.

"Richie not only owned the Black Bears, but also the Jack Rabbits. He offered to sell me a percentage of the team, with league approval."

To qualify, Geoff needed a big name to join him.

"A friend of mine introduced me to Jeremy Lin."

Jeremy agreed to invest in the team, and they renamed it the Bay Area Breakers. The team is now in its third season.

Geoff loves the game and how it brings people together.

"Basically, everybody that I've met in my recent life is through the sport of pickleball and through the community it creates."

He continues, "One of the cool things about the Bay Area Breakers, and Jeremy Lin being based in the Bay, is that it gives us an opportunity to build a community around this brand that we have."

"We always bring the team out to the community. One of the exciting things about being at the beginning of this league is seeing how fast it's growing."

The team often does exhibitions and even plays with the fans.

"One of the cool things I've noticed is that the pickleball scene actually isn't as big as we're seeing it out in Austin and Florida, or even here in Southern California. There's not a ton of places to play."

Currently, the team's biggest fan base is mostly Jeremy Lin fans.

Says Geoff, "We have a strong Instagram following, and it gets the fans more interested in pickleball."

Geoff knows that challenges still exist between the amateur side and the professional game.

"The recreational players don't cross over as much as we would like. So, if you're an amateur playing pickleball, how likely is it that you're going to also follow the professional pickleball world?"

"We go to facilities all over the Bay Area and introduce the game at the grassroots level," says Geoff.

"It still surprises me today when I visit a facility and we talk to them about professional pickleball, and they actually have no idea what it is."

Another important focus for Geoff is Pickleball Cares (https://www.pickleballcares.org/).

"When Steve Kuhn was the CEO of Major League Pickleball, he approached me about how to bring the sport of pickleball to kids, but was never able to get it up and running."

Geoff decided it was something he wanted to take on and created the nonprofit.

Since its inception, Pickleball Cares has been introducing the game to children in underserved communities.

"We did a clinic in Oakland, brought in temporary nets, taped the courts, and had donated equipment from companies like Joola and Selkirk."

Geoff knows the importance of spending time with friends and playing sports.

"We are introducing kids to something that brings them outside and away from their phones."

Pickleball Cares knows the importance of getting kids moving again.

Says Geoff, "Too many are on their computers, on their phones, and playing games. Pickleball is really helping with their mental health, also, and not just their physical health."

Geoff sees a lot of unique individuals playing the sport.

"Did you know that Ben Johns (professional player) is also an avid Fortnite gamer?"

"The best thing about Pickleball Cares is all of these kids walk away with a paddle, and they make some friends at the clinic. Hopefully, they will continue to play and share the sport with others," says Geoff.

"We are seeing a lot more pickleball in elementary, middle and high schools and even some universities."

Pickleball Cares now has programming across the country.

"The easiest way for us to access kids is through the leagues. So, the MLP and PPA host tournaments across the country, allowing us to bring kids from the various communities to our free clinics," says Geoff.

"We work with other organizations like the YMCA, the Just Keep Living Foundation (Matthew McConaughey), and the Drew Brees Dream Foundation."

"When we launched, most of the Major League Pickleball teams donated money to the League or to the Foundation. Everybody was very generous."

In the first year, Geoff's organization was able to raise over half a million dollars.

"Since then, we've had some teams continue to contribute on a monthly basis. But the idea is we would hope that the league continues to contribute on an annual basis."

Individuals and small businesses are now also stepping up and helping to fuel new funding.

Geoff continues to see great collaboration in the sport.

"So, I'll use Atlanta as an example. One of the largest sponsors for the PPA is Veolia, the sustainability company with who we partnered to do a clinic. The kids spent half of the time learning about sustainability, and the other half playing pickleball."

"Another great resource has been the hundreds of players from the league. They have been very generous to us and allow the players to come and instruct these clinics on a volunteer basis."

Geoff continues, "I have a good relationship with most of the players on tour."

Spending lots of time together, most are very happy about donating their time to support the kids.

Looking ahead, Geoff continues to put great effort into professional pickleball.

"With the MLP and PPA competing for the same player base, our revenue is not yet equal to our expenses. At some point, salaries will need to be adjusted for the sport to succeed."

"The sport continues to surprise me. I mean, look at CJ Klinger who plays at such a high level and just won a gold medal at the Atlanta PPA. And he's only 18."

Geoff continues, "And former tennis player Jessie Irvine had to leave the professional tennis tour because of her injury issues because it was limiting her mobility. But being able to transition to pickleball has changed her life because now she can continue playing a sport professionally."

"There is even a general manager of one of the NBA teams who comes to my house to play pickleball. He tells me how players are always looking for courts to play on and cross-train."

Geoff continues, "And ref Scott Foster is a huge pickleball player. During the season, he's always looking for courts as he travels during the season."

Geoff loves how the game brings such unique people together.

"Now you're associating with a lot of different people and different backgrounds that you wouldn't have otherwise."

He continues, "If you look at human dynamics, youth tend to stay with youth, older tend to stay with older. And as you move through life, you tend to get into your little pods. But when you walk out of a pickleball court, it's any age, any size, and the diversity is insane."

Gordon Gebert

Rockin' on the Pickleball Court

It all started during a visit to his parents' house in Florida when Gordon was first introduced to pickleball.

"My brother tells me we are going to play. I had no idea what he was talking about," Gordon recalls.

Walking onto the courts, he watched a solid game between some 3.5 level players.

"They were pretty good. I caught on fast."

"When I got back to Connecticut, I had to Google pickleball."

Gordon found a local coach named Betsy Underhill and asked her to teach him.

"She had no idea I was on a mission to get really good, real fast. I wanted to go back to Florida and kick my brother's ass."

Growing up as a baseball pitcher, Gordon loved all sports.

"I played football, basketball, and even tennis. Tennis legend Vitas Gerulaitis taught me how to serve."

No matter the sport, Gordon and his brother were always competing.

"It's so weird how addictive pickleball is. All you have to do is touch a paddle," says Gordon.

"For me, it's the perfect paddle game out there."

He soon went on Amazon, bought the cheapest paddle he could find, and started playing.

"I still have it. I'm not really much of a paddle freak today. I would play with a frying pan."

"All I knew was that I didn't want to go to the gym, so I played pickleball. Exercise is my thing."

Gordon continues, "My wheelhouse is three hours. Other guys, they'll play an hour and a half, two hours, and then they're wiped. But I've had days where I played six hours straight, and everybody's going, how are you doing it?"

A world-touring rock musician, Gordon had been searching for a new passion.

"I was probably a little lost after playing with famous bands. That was my life."

His career as a keyboardist put him on the stage and working with legends like Keith Emerson, Liberty Devitto (Billy Joel), Marty Balin, Motley Crue, and Ace Frehley.

Now an accomplished player, Gordon is also a certified pickleball instructor.

"So I coached the president of JetBlue. He lived in the area and picked up a ball. I didn't know who he was."

Says Gordon, "I love the game, which to me is more like chess. I really approach it like a musician. I love playing live, improvising and doing jams. If done right, it can be a magical performance."

"When you are playing doubles, and don't know what your partner will do, you have to improvise. The game is constantly moving, you are constantly thinking, and the stage is constantly changing."

For Gordon, it's the rhythm of the hits that helps him play better.

"Being a musician, it's a subconscious thing for me."

One memorable experience was playing at Ivan Lendl's tennis facility in Bedford, NY, where he met pro player Ken Henderson (the 2018 singles champ).

"I got my butt kicked, but he asked me to stick around."

Gordon shared his new concept for a training paddle.

"Ken thought it was a great idea and encouraged me to finish it."

From that conversation, The Slam Master (https://slammaster.net/about) was born.

Now teaching, Gordon loves to share the strategy of the game with the help of his custom paddle.

"Anyone who tries it understands that they really weren't watching the ball. But with my Slam Master, their hand-eye coordination immediately improves, helping the ball get over the net with accuracy and power."

"I'm always thinking, 'Put pressure on the other side'. The Slam Master has developed all my mechanics and made everything quicker."

Gordon continues, "Just days ago, I played with some guys who couldn't believe how good I was."

Playing rec games constantly, Gordon would find himself in multiple locations almost every day.

"I would go to one place in the morning, another in the afternoon, and another in the evening."

His friends worried Gordon would get burned out or even injured.

"I couldn't stop, as I was just obsessed with playing."

"So, I joined a couple of local leagues and stuff. And I hated the models. They were too restrictive with player matches, reporting, and match duration."

Not a fan of DUPR, Gordon knew there had to be a better way.

"I developed the NPL (https://usa-npl.com/) so you could record your rec game scores."

The league has gone national with season tournaments, rankings, and prizes.

"I have 1,800 players in the program with no advertising."

With over 50 Ambassadors, Gordon knows this is just the start.

"This year, it's going to grow exponentially. I give my ambassadors all the credit."

Gordon has seen his social circle explode around pickleball.

"In music, I worked with the guys from KISS, so I learned from the best."

That experience has helped Gordon build the NPL.

"Being in music has helped me develop a rhythm for business and also take my brand knowledge and use it in the pickleball world."

One of his funniest stories happened while playing.

Said Gordon, "I always put a camera up to watch my games and analyze them. Some don't like it, and I always ask before recording."

He continues, "I got hit square in the face by a really good player. Earlier that day, I had heard they were targeting me, which I'm fine with."

"The other guys were talking smack, asking if I had brought a Kevlar suit. Being silly, my friend said that anyone who could hit me would get five bucks."

Being ultra-competitive and not afraid of strong shots, Gordon was ready for anything.

"I got hit straight in the nose when my opponent smashed an overhead at me."

The video ended up going viral and was clipped a bit for effect.

"The comments are so hysterical!"

Gordon is fully aware of the pickleball fever that's happening.

"There are guys trying to make millions of dollars with pickleball, trying to fast track it into tennis and a spectator sport."

He continues, "It's not a spectator sport right now. Who wants to sit and watch pickleball for hours? It's still a grassroots business."

Spending so much time on recreational courts, Gordon knows that the game is still trying to catch up to itself.

"Most people don't know the names of any players on the tour except Ben Johns. And that's only because his name is on a paddle."

Pickleball has even led to unexpected reunions.

"So, one day I'm playing pickleball at a court about 45 minutes away," says Gordon.

"I hear this guy on the other side with a French Italian accent, and it's my old friend Maurice from music who I hadn't seen in years!"

He continues, "Much had changed, including my hair, which was once down to my butt. We spent almost every day together at my house recording music. What a great surprise!"

On a trip to Maine, Gordon met up with a new friend named Rocky Clark who picked him up to play at a local court.

"The passenger seat was taken, so I got into the back of the car. Both were in the middle of a conversation, so I was not introduced. I didn't know who it was until he turned around."

Says Gordon, "It was Prem Carnot, the Pickleball Guru. He was one of the first guys to endorse my Slam Master paddle. Another fantastic surprise!"

"I was in Delray Beach doing a tournament, and I bought a booth with my buddy Coach Z (Zorano Tubo). It's during COVID and we are demonstrating the Slam Master."

Still having to mask up, the duo was situated near the front where the players walk in.

"The pros would walk by laughing at me and making comments about the toy in my hand."

Sales that weekend were strong, as many rec players who tried it bought it. But the pro players ignored it.

Going back the next year, Gordon got one of the pros to stop and try it out.

"I'm showing him how to use it, and he couldn't do what I did."

Says Gordon, "After some awkward tries, he started to master its uses up to a volley."

The player, Scott Moore, left to go play in the tournament.

"Soon after, he returned and told me he won the gold in a volley war. I was so happy when he said the paddle had helped."

Gordon continues, "A week and a half later, Scott endorsed the paddle and asked to do a deal. He uses it all the time and sells them to his clients at his clinics. I have to give him lots of credit for my success."

Gordon loves the social aspect of pickleball.

"It's really cool. I mean, I get to meet all these unbelievable people in my celebrity world. I just went out to LA to try and get a game with Brett Michaels from Poison, because he just built a pickleball court on his property."

He continues, "I've played with Kyle Yates, Rob Cassidy and even Colin Johns. I should quit pickleball, because you can't get any better than that."

Jared Bonner

Pickleheads

"I remember back in grade school or middle school, we played pickleball for two weeks, and everybody had a blast. Then it just disappeared until my parents started playing in 2020 during COVID."

Jared continues, "My parents were playing with their friends down the road and invited me. I was beating everyone up and didn't know if it was because I was good, or they weren't."

His parents' 55-plus community has a great pickleball scene now.

"So many people come from racquetball and other sports and are technically sound. Age doesn't really matter."

Jared also knows you can't judge a book by its cover.

"Everybody's got their little niche or some side spin that you haven't seen before. It's a pretty great game to get people moving and talking."

"Pickleball is a good way to connect and meet new people and play with some pros to see where your game is at," says Jared.

"I love the flexibility too, where you don't need to set a time. You can almost walk in any city in the country and find a game. I definitely can't do that in golf or tennis. You can show up and leave when you want. It's fascinating that it's a 15, 20 minute-ish kind of experience that just duplicates."

"Right after COVID, I shot a movie, and I gained 30 pounds because I thought it was funny to play a single dad in a dance team movie called 'Dance Dads.'"

Jared had trouble losing weight.

"It started bothering me because it wasn't coming off, even with me exercising and dieting. Nothing was working."

Two years later, Jared started playing more with friends as the sport started to gain popularity.

"There are a few courts here in Austin, and I just got addicted and jumped in 100 percent."

Soon after a breakup, Jared started playing religiously and cut back on his drinking.

"Within two months, I lost 30 pounds and was back to normal. I was like, Ooh, I guess I just needed to find a sport and something that didn't feel like cardio."

He continues, "It kind of saved me, and soon after that I met my now pregnant wife."

Growing up playing soccer and basketball, Jared loves the lateral movement of the game, where he can show off his deceptive speed.

"Since then, I've just been learning, drilling, and working with new people. And it's been a blast."

Now a 4.5 player, he competes in about four tournaments a year.

No matter where you are, there are always games to be found.

"I can be in Tulsa visiting my in-laws, and head over to Lifetime to play. It's great to just get a little sweat in and play with some new people with new skills."

Jared also loves how the game doesn't get too political.

"I don't care who anybody voted for. And I feel like this is what brings people together because no one is talking about politics or about things going on in the news, which can be crippling to a lot of conversations."

"It's interesting how this game is different from golf, but it's the same as golf, but it just has a much wider footprint to it. A lot of people who do business don't play golf, but they do play pickleball."

Jared sets up games with investors and producers for not only a business meeting, but also to get the blood flowing.

"It helps people get comfortable and adds an ease to tough conversations."

"My feature film, Pickleheads, is a mockumentary comedy," says Jared.

"I think a grassroots sport like this needs a narrative film, an underdog film to put it in the market and get people attached to."

He continues, "It's about getting people to laugh at themselves."

"In one scene, there's a turf war or rumble between pickleball and tennis players."

"The feature is writing itself. While researching the film, I found a lot of protests and turf wars over concrete slabs, which I find hysterical. People either love the game or hate it. Either way, there's lots of love going around."

Jared sees a huge void of entertainment around pickleball themes.

"There's such a demand and need in the market. And what I do is connect people through comedy, writing, and the characters."

Growing up in the nineties, his work was heavily influenced by movies like *Happy Gilmore*, *Dodgeball*, *Hot Rod* and *Kingpin*.

"I miss those comedies and I'm on a mission to get them back."

"'Pickleheads' was shot like *The Office*, like a mockumentary, following this underdog. My hero always seems to be a man that's pretty broken and lost, looking to find his purpose."

The logline reads:"After a mid-match shart heard around the world ends his ping pong career in global disgrace, Barney Bardot vanishes into the woods to live the life of a sasquatch. Nine years later, his debt-ridden half-brother drags him back to society to help save their family home by conquering America's fastest growing sport, Pickleball."

The all-star cast turned out to get the hang of the sport quickly.

"Even never having touched a paddle before, the lead actress Kristine Froseth did a great job of listening, reacting, and pushing it forward."

"The archrival who plays Hawkeye, Eric Nelson, was an *1883* actor and in a western thriller I wrote called *Cottonmouth* with me."

Jared knew he had a pickleball court in his backyard.

"Eric shows up ready to drill and clearly knows how to play."

Rounding out the cast was Lindsey Morgan.

Says Jared, "Playing ping pong all the time on family vacations, she got the hang of it right away. All we had to teach her were the rules."

The movie even had support from The Austin Pickle Ranch and owner Tim Klitch.

"We had two trainers come in and play with us. It really helped the pickleball play and getting some actual points. Of course, the movie is definitely a mockumentary comedy first and sports drama second."

"As inclusive as a sport is, I wanted to make it as PG as possible," says Jared.

"But it still has some PG-13 moments, like people bleeped out cursing, you know, things like that."

He continues, "We want to do experiential releases before the movie comes out streaming and kind of build an audience around it. So, we want to travel across the country, maybe do eight to ten big pickleball venues that people can invite their families to."

With pickleball still in its infancy, Jared sees the movie as a great vehicle to help grow the sport.

"A lot of recreational players don't know about Major League Pickleball or the PPA."

He continues, "I'm really trying to connect both pro and rec play and build the sport as well as make people laugh in the theater."

Jared is excited about the upcoming release.

"The movie is turning out so well. And I just want to be the first narrative film to kind of hit the market. And we're in a prime position to really knock it out of the park."

He continues, "We hope to kind of keep *Pickleheads* going and do a sequel. There's a possibility to take it international if it continues to grow in other countries like Spain and Australia, where it's getting pretty big."

"I hope *Pickleheads* becomes the next *Rocky Horror* or *Caddyshack* or some combo between the two," says Jared.

"How great would it be for everyone to be talking about the movie, laughing their ass off, then going to play pickleball because they love the game even more?"

Jared Paul

The Kitchen

Starting his career in sales, Jared moved all over the country. "When I turned 30, I decided to leave the corporate world and started a nonprofit helping the homeless members of the community in the Bay Area."

Jared did that for about five years.

"It kind of transitioned me from sales to marketing and community building."

Soon realizing he was unemployable, Jared started a music blog and met his current co-founder at Coachella.

"We launched a free ticket marketplace on Facebook, and that helped bring us to The Kitchen."

Moving from the Bay Area to Austin to raise a round of funding for a music startup, Jared's plans came to a crashing halt with the start of the pandemic.

"That June, a buddy invited me to play pickleball. I had never heard of it and instantly fell in love with the sport."

Says Jared, "We ended up playing regularly at places like Bolden Acres and the South Austin Rec Center."

"I wrestled in high school and was mildly athletic, but not super athletic. I think that's why pickleball is so popular."

Jared continues, "All of us who didn't compete in a high school sport now have the opportunity to do it here."

On a visit to Dude Perfect's headquarters in Frisco to play pickleball, Jared and his partner, Dane were immediately inspired.

"They are big influencers in sports. We left there thinking how cool it would be to have some version of their business in our own way."

Soon, the team came across a space and decided to go with it.

Says Jared, "It was going to be more of an event space, even though we haven't hosted many since. We have done a bunch of our own, like hosting a big MLP kickoff party (they own a team), and it's been awesome."

"It's our private place to play, hang out, and work," says Jared.

The facility has its own court, its own bar and even a podcast studio where they recently recorded their second episode.

"We are super excited about that!"

"I'm on my phone constantly because of work or my computer, way too much. When I'm outside and away from my phone, it's mainly because of pickleball. I think it's a great way to get away from technology and connect with people," says Jared.

"I would say we are pickleball diehards who created this community to bring people together and deliver high-value content that others weren't doing at the time," says Jared.

The team's greatest asset is their Facebook community.

"We have about 165,000 diehard players in it. Our polling showed that 80% of them play four days a week or more."

Jared continues, "This is where everything trickles down."

Including their Instagram channel, The Kitchen has almost 1.5 million followers, members, and email subscribers.

"We believe in organic marketing and have spent less than $10,000 to build our following."

Last month, their efforts reached 120 million people across all channels, giving them the greatest reach in the industry.

Says Jared, "It's a mix of the pickleball diehard in us, blending culture and pickleball."

With only four employees, The Kitchen relies on an ambassador program.

Jared says, "It's not like a formal ambassador program. We just keep focusing on doing great stuff to help us grow."

Their podcast is a great example.

"We spent several months planning it before launching the first episode because we want to do it right."

"That's kind of the philosophy of everything we put out there. We want it to look and feel great," says Jared.

"I still do all of our social media posts. Like yesterday, I spent probably an hour on one highlight video just finding the right song and syncing it up. And sometimes it works, and sometimes it doesn't. But I think that attention to detail is seen and felt."

The team has done work with celebrities like Drew Brees, Jamie Foxx, and Rob Gronkowski.

"We go to big events; we do this thing on Necker Island with Richard Branson. But really, I think it's just that we're tapped into the pro scene, we're tapped into the amateur scene. And 90% of what we do is really tailored to the amateurs, which make up 99% of the sport," says Jared.

"I think pickleball is absolutely changing lives. We just did a story documenting how playing a sport like pickleball leads to a 60% reduction in depression."

Jared also knows how important the social aspect is.

"The social circle that I've met around the country is pretty crazy. And I think most who play the game are building their community from it."

Jared knows the importance of bringing people together.

"I think community is super important, getting off the computer and connecting and going outside."

He continues, "I'd like to think that on the content side, we're providing entertainment and joy and laughter. We're educating people. And through events, we're bringing people together."

"I think it's going to become the largest participatory sport in the world," says Jared.

"It brings people together. It's highly democratized. You can go out for the first time and have a good time. It's a sport that also takes a lifetime to master."

"Pickleball has become a huge part of people's identity," he says.

"For the most part, I'd say it's a very healthy addiction, although I do know some marriages that have ended because of that."

Jared continues, "I think 50% of orthopedic surgeons' patients are coming from pickleball. So, there's definitely a downside. But I would say for the most part, it's changing lives and becoming a fabric of society."

Jared loves how pickleball has reconnected him to old friends.

"We had a Georgia vs. Texas football pregame party here, and there's a bunch of people from high school who loved how cool the venue was."

He continues, "On a visit to Atlanta, I connected with a kid from my little league baseball team who I played in a band with in high school. I hadn't seen him in like 25 years. He loves playing pickleball, so we just hung out and talked about the game and our lives."

Pickleball has even become part of the music industry.

"James Valentine from Maroon 5 is a huge pickleball guy," says Jared.

"I've seen other bands post videos of them playing before gigs. One of them was at Red Rocks. I have even seen Dua Lipa and Justin Bieber are now playing pickleball. There's a ton playing."

"One of the challenges with pickleball is figuring out how to get people who play for their first time and really like it," says Jared.

"Now they need to become part of a community of people who have similar skill levels. I think in some ways we're doing a good job, but in others we can do better. Like, how can we help foster that journey for them?"

It's a question he continues to ask his team.

"I think it's our responsibility to provide value and just inform and educate. We want to provide moments where people can get on the court and play pickleball."

Travel continues to be a big part of his work.

"I've traveled quite a bit, probably more than I'd like to quite honestly. We went to Peru for the Pickleball World Cup last year. We went to Necker Island twice. We've been all over the country for tournaments."

"The team is even working with Airbnbs with pickleball courts they can stay at while traveling."

"Time is now my biggest hurdle," says Jared.

"My calendar is just jammed with tournaments and business trips. It's just non-stop."

Recently invited to experience a trip on a yacht in Croatia, Jared had to decline.

"I love Croatia, but literally have no time left right now."

Jared knows the pro game has a long way to go.

"We work with the PPA and MLP, supporting them every way possible. But I think the TV experience can improve, as the game doesn't translate well."

Jared knows that gaining more corporate sponsors will be key to long-term success.

"It'll be fun to see where it's at in five years."

As the GM of the Nashville Chefs Major League Pickleball team, Jared is in constant motion.

"Our team plays a role in the management of the Chefs and our own large-scale amateur tournaments."

This year, they have hosted events with hundreds of players and thousands of spectators.

Growing up an Atlanta Falcons fan, Drew Brees was a nemesis to Jared.

"My experience with Drew has been pretty amazing. I connected with him at an MLP event, and he agreed to do this content series called Lunch Game with us and flew out to San Diego. And we played Drew, and this other pro."

Jared remembers it vividly.

"It was one of those 'pinch myself' moments wondering how did I get here?"

The two even got to play a pickleball match on Necker Island.

"So 'Rise Up' is a big Falcons saying," said Jared.

"Right before we started playing, I said it to Drew. Even though it was a close match, we lost."

The two had become friendly during the game and Jared got invited to fly back on his private jet from Necker Island.

Wiped from an active week on the island, all the passengers on the flight fell asleep except for Drew and Jared.

"It was pretty surreal. We stayed up kind of talking about life and football and pickleball for what felt like eight hours. So that was pretty cool."

On a trip to Palm Springs, Jared was invited to meet up with Jamie Foxx.

"On our way there, we are driving down the street in this insane neighborhood and Phil Knight is just walking down the street. And we were like, wow, like, how did we get invited to Jamie Foxx's house? It was crazy."

"Jamie showed up late, and we missed our flight. But we didn't care."

Jared continues, "He's decked out in a big puffy jacket. It was super-hot out at the time. Jamie tells us he's down to play but we have to have lunch first. There was no way we were going to pass up that offer, even if we missed our flight. And so, we go up and he has his chefs making us this insane meal and we're hanging out popping bottles of champagne. So crazy!"

Says Jared, "There are so many fun memories of hanging out with friends and playing in different cities. It's really become an integral part of all my travels."

Jared knows pickleball is the fastest growing sport in the country.

"It's a sport that anyone can go out and have fun playing but doesn't take a lifetime to master. To me, it's like the perfect sport of being social and exercising."

"My brother and I used to play pickleball and we're highly competitive. I play with my wife and have even started throwing balls to my daughter who's almost five. It would be really cool to see her play."

Jared loves the family dynamics.

"It's intergenerational. Even though we don't play as much together as a family, I still love how this aspect of the game has helped the sport skyrocket."

Jay "Gizmo" Hall
Pickleball Farm

Jay was introduced to pickleball in 2018. "I was at a rec center just shooting around and heard this sound on the other side of the gym."

Thinking it was ping pong, he went down to check it out.

"Peeking around the corner, I saw three nets set up and a bleacher full of older people. I had no idea what was going on."

He was soon approached by a lady. Says Jay, "She's like, you know, this is pickleball. Would you like me to show you how it works? I said no and just watched."

A few days later Jay returned to the gym.

"I'm shooting around again and I hear that same exact sound and I do the exact same thing, peek around that corner and those same two ladies come up to me and they grab me by the hand and they say, 'You don't get to look twice without at least trying it once.'"

Handed a paddle, Jay was taken onto the court.

"They showed me how to play the game. I can't believe I was introduced to pickleball by two 70-year-old ladies."

From that moment, Jay knew there was something special about the game.

"Six months later, I ended up quitting my job at the fire department I was working at to chase this crazy dream and become a professional pickleball player."

"So, it's crazy, man. The evolution of this sport since 2018 has been eye-opening on so many levels. I mean the growth has been exponential."

Says Jay, "Year after year, it's becoming the fastest growing sport in America."

He knows everyone picks up the game for different reasons.

"For me personally, I'm more focused on the community aspect."

Jay has seen the life-changing potential of pickleball.

"As I have transitioned out of playing tournaments, it's allowed me to focus on giving the game to the juvenile detention facilities, the school systems, and the average guy or girl out on the pickleball court who may have never even thought that there was an opportunity to go professional in the sport," he said.

"I still play a few tournaments a year, but traveling two to three weeks a month on tour again just lost its luster for me."

"I feel like I can be more impactful on this front doing the type of work that I do now. I've got two kids, a beautiful wife. I've got a 10-acre farm in Virginia. Coming from what I grew up with, which was little to nothing to what I have now, I'm okay with that, so long as I'm able to still spread the word of pickleball till the day I die because of how impactful it was to me."

When Jay and his wife bought their farm, they had to come up with a name.

"I told her 'Pickleball Farm' and she said no way!"

After hearing Jay out, they settled on the name.

"Our mission overall is pickleball. Even though we both still have regular jobs, we can continue to build up the farm."

"Pickleball Farm was created to provide the youth and families of the community with the opportunity to learn where our food comes from, how to garden, and of course play pickleball," says Jay.

"All crops grown at Pickleball Farm are donated to the local food bank or another non-profit that donates fresh produce to families in need."

Through a successful fundraising campaign, the couple was able to build a permanent pickleball court.

Says Jay, "We bring kids, families, and groups out, and teach them pickleball. We've got chickens, turkeys, goats, pigs, and a mini donkey. We introduce them to the livestock. They can feed them. And then we've also got a USDA grant to get a 1,600 square foot greenhouse. So our goal every year is to grow and donate 5,000 pounds of produce and teach 5,000 kids the game of pickleball."

"Whether by word of mouth, going into the school systems, the juvenile detention facilities, or having kids come out here, our goal is to share the game with as many as possible," he said.

"It will be a night and day difference in my opinion. With what we've undertaken here, it doesn't matter if kids want to fish at the pond, go feed apples to the chickens or turkeys, or get their hands dirty in the soil and plant some potatoes. We just surround them with love and, of course, introduce them to pickleball while they're here. We've received nothing but great feedback from that."

Jay and his wife continue to make a lot of progress.

"We were recently down in Florida at the Southwest Florida Juvenile Detention Center and got to paint pickleball courts on their outdoor space."

He continues, "To my knowledge, that was the first in the nation to actually do that. And it's just been amazing, the feedback that we've gotten, because again, at the end of the day, the one glaring thing with youth that I found is kids just need something to occupy their time."

"I was fortunate enough to go down to Mexico and go to a school and teach pickleball to a bunch of fifth and sixth graders."

Using translators, Jay found a way to connect with the children.

"I was still able to get across the basics of the sport of pickleball and to see the kids go from not knowing how to hold the paddle and just smacking balls all around chasing balls to actually playing points out."

The experience opened his eyes.

"The trip gave me lots of validity to what I was doing," said Jay.

"Just being able to introduce a demographic who may or may not have ever heard of pickleball was amazing. Because of the rapid growth of the game, some will be left behind. Heck, I was 31 before I ever heard of the sport."

Jay has been able to bring pickleball into urban areas where tennis courts were in ruin.

"I visited Woodbridge, Virginia where there were four tennis courts in the same parking lot as one of the police precincts. The nets were ripped down, and it just wasn't a good place to be."

Through his efforts, things changed.

Says Jay, "We converted four tennis courts to eight pickleball courts. And I would be lying if I said that those courts aren't jam-packed from sunup to sundown."

"Pickleball gets people out to socialize and exercise. That's the draw to the sport. This umbrella is easy to grab. And if we can create more pockets like that, it means that there's less pockets for the more evils of the world," Jay said.

It's hard to find someone else more passionate about sharing the game.

"I don't ever want somebody to be able to say that they weren't introduced to the sport of pickleball based on them not being able to afford it," says Jay.

"You know, us pickleball snobs will complain about a $4 ball all day long. But somebody just getting introduced to the game couldn't care if they were hitting with a jugs ball, a Selkirk ball, a Dura 40, a Franklin, a Lifetime," he said.

"Paddles make no difference to them. You can spend upwards of $300 on a paddle, but I think at Walmart I saw one for ten or twelve bucks. All you need is a flat surface or a parking lot. I've even seen it played on clay courts."

Says Jay, "Think about all the people who will be introduced to pickleball now who maybe have never heard of it? They can then go in with a super low barrier cost of entry by spending 40 bucks on a set of paddles and a few balls."

He continues, "It's one of the only sports that's also multi-generational. You know, a lot of times you see grandparents out there playing with grandkids. There's not many other sports that come to mind with that same correlation."

"It's almost like you're living in two different worlds here. One is to come to our house, come to our farm, come to our community. The second one is, let me bring you this game. Let me bring you this experience. Let me bring you the chance to get others around you to play."

"I'm a big fan of not trying to reinvent the wheel," says Jay.

"Once I started doing what I was doing with the youth, I think I may have seen somebody post something on Pickleball Forum within the last couple of years."

He continues, "I was like, man, that dude has got it figured out!"

Jay often sees others look down on the prison population.

"They see us go in and think we are in harm's way. But all the prisoners earn the right to try pickleball, it's not something just any hardened criminal can do."

"Now I'm focused on bringing it to the juvenile facilities. The game translates there by the connection made from playing," says Jay.

"A lot of times I have people call or text me to learn more about what I'm doing. I tell them it always starts by treating everyone with respect, because I was once in the same spot they are. Not many people even know I was shot four times."

Given a new lease on life, Jay has since started a family, bought a farm, become a professional pickleball player, and started a Foundation.

"I would have never, ever been able to think that that was an option until I saw somebody who quite honestly looked like me or had been through something that I had been through that was able to make a connection to even begin a conversation with me."

Jay has often been asked about racism in pickleball.

"My immediate response is that the people who play pickleball are the same people that exist in the world. So yes."

He continues, "I don't care what you look like. I don't care what your gender is. I don't care how tall you are. I don't care how fat you are. I don't care what medical conditions you have. I don't care what your political beliefs are. If you want to hit this plastic ball over this net inside of these white lines, we'll call it good."

But Jay has also experienced it.

"I've also shown up to facilities to play tournaments and stopped at the front desk and asked somebody where the pickleball courts are? And they look at me and say, basketball courts? I said, no, no ma'am. I was asking for the pickleball courts."

"I just focus on the now and focus on who I can help. Every day I wake up as a man on a mission and here to serve."

Jay continues, "So I have to ask myself, how can I serve? Whether it be through growing food to donate, whether it be through having families or groups come out to Pickleball Farm, or whether it be through me going somewhere to speak. I just keep trying to figure out how to make the biggest impact I can."

Jay continues to see the game in Fire Departments across the United States.

"They are pulling the engines out of the bays and lining courts, so it's definitely picking up."

This summer, Jay will go down to the World Police and Fire Games in Birmingham, Alabama to play pickleball.

"I don't know where I would have been if I didn't get introduced to pickleball," says Jay.

"I had just lost my mother. I was spiraling out of control mental health wise. I was probably going to leave the fire department without a plan. But it's crazy how everything happens for a reason."

Jay still speaks to the ladies who introduced him to the game.

"I still go to the same Rec Center a couple of times a year and play with them, and they love it. They absolutely love it."

He continues, "We had absolutely nothing else in common. I can guarantee it. They saved my life, and so did the game of pickleball."

Jodi Cullity

From Global Stages to Pickleball Courts

In 2022, Jodi's life was radically changed. "I was working at the White House after living in Dubai and remember sitting at the UN General Assembly in New York City."

She remembers feeling a gap of fulfillment and only wished to be with her parents and local community, playing pickleball.

"That was my jump to entrepreneurship."

Jodi always wanted to be an entrepreneur, now the time felt right.

"The human connection I felt on the pickleball court was just something that I craved every day. And I saw how transformative it was for my community."

And that is where the opportunity of the brick-and-mortar kind of fell onto Jodi's lap while networking with the Head of Construction at Gillette Stadium.

"For two years I was a pickleball consultant and worked hard to understand this business vertical."

Jodi went all in, visiting over 60 facilities domestically and internationally.

"I put my paws in almost everything from Major League Pickleball to PPA to international pickleball tournaments."

Jodi continues, "I'm really just in love with the growth of the industry and how it's booming. I would definitely say my entrepreneurship journey is not just our brick and mortar."

Growing up a competitive athlete, pickleball helped reawaken that spirit.

"I definitely am more of a social pickleball player. It was so nice to regain a community feel with the game post pandemic. I hadn't felt that since my younger years in sports."

On a government trip in Barcelona, Spain, Jodi was on a layover and decided to stay a few days.

"I'm not into touristy things and wanted to play pickleball."

So, she hopped a train to the only facility she knew of, which was 30 minutes outside of the city.

"Two years ago, it was called Vila Pickleball and was the only place in Europe."

"No one in the facility spoke English and I just wanted to play," said Jodi.

"So, we all got on the court and had the absolute best time. Everyone had to use Google translate on their phone to communicate."

From this, she gained a whole new set of friends.

"For me, knowing the international landscape of sports diplomacy is so important."

Jodi knows firsthand how sports break down any type of political or international affairs differences.

"I saw it firsthand, because I travel so much. With a pickleball paddle, I can show up in any country to teach or play the game."

She continues, "I played in Kenya. They didn't even know what pickleball was. It's so amazing to be able to share a sport with someone that only takes a couple of minutes to learn."

"So, we (https://www.eleveno.com/) are at a campus at Gillette Stadium. Our main location is Patriot Place, which is the retail arm outside of the stadium."

Jodi loves the natural connection to the stadium.

"Running our pop-ups on campus, we had a lot of interest from visiting pro sports teams, whether they were soccer teams playing the Revolution or the wives and girlfriends of the Patriots, they would naturally just trickle into our facility."

Being part of the Patriots' footprint, Jodi quickly made key connections.

"I met Dante Scarnecchia (former coach) playing at ForeKicks. He's become our local celebrity."

This friendship helped open doors to many more in the Patriots family, including Josh McDaniels (offensive coach).

"I think we're just a really young industry still, even with Major League Pickleball. We have a really great opportunity as an American sport to make it the next MLS, NBA or NFL."

Says Jodi, "I'm very excited to be part of an industry that's American driven because our sports fan base is unlike anything else in the world."

Jodi knows the industry is often referred to as the Wild West.

"That's what makes pickleball so special. We have the opportunity unlike a lot of different industries to start something from scratch."

She continues, "I find that every pickleball executive, owner or player I meet is very entrepreneurial. Everyone wants this sport to boom. We haven't had an industry with this much momentum in a very long time."

"From a design perspective and our build out, we're really trying to showcase not only the personality of our team, but the personality of our players that walk in. So, we really want them to feel like they have ownership in our facility," says Jodi.

"Maybe they'll only come once or twice, but it's almost like a bucket list item. Have you been to ELEVENO? Did you sign that wall?"

Jodi started the company with her parents in mind.

"My dad is a retired firefighter. My mom is an elementary school bus driver. Neither are country club people. They are not tennis people."

She continues, "They even felt very timid going to the free public courts because they just said they've never played the sport before. My parents are very frugal and are my core customer, and every decision goes through them. Because if I can't appease them, then I know people won't spend the money."

"My parents then really shifted into becoming entrepreneurs. They give me a lot of different ideas," says Jodi.

"My mom's working on a pickleball puzzle and pickleball card deck and graphic design. It's really inspired a lot in my family to come into the business."

"My whole goal with ELEVENO was to create that hospitable, welcoming atmosphere above all else," Jodi says.

"We work with sponsors specifically to make our everyday athlete feel like a VIP. Every time you sign up for any of our programs and you walk in our facility, you get something for free. We like to go the extra mile in making sure that our players feel really welcome."

"We do a lot with pickleball programs as well as with the special needs and integration program at the YMCA, which helps us to be more creative," says Jodi.

"Instead of a traditional game, we play Red Rover with pickleball and do an egg toss bringing us back to our camp counselor days," She said.

"With all of our pop-up tournaments in the past, we've always had activities around the court because after playing a few hours we want them to stay, to eat and drink and mingle with each other."

The facility has had a lot of people show up alone to play.

"Being at Gillette Stadium, we do see a lot of travelers. And so they're in town for work or they're in town for the big game and they don't know anyone," says Jodi.

"So, these activities are easy icebreakers for more socializing. Very similar to Topgolf, we are hospitality-driven first, with competition always second. We hope to be the largest flagship in New England."

Jodi is excited to see some colleges offering scholarships for pickleball.

"I think the investment that towns are putting in for public courts around America is really impressive. And that's where the accessibility of the player demographic will continue to grow."

"We've seen grocery store pickleball pop-ups. We've seen Formula One pickleball pop-ups," says Jodi.

"But I think the most impactful ones are going to continue to be when pickleball trickles down into the school system, becomes an official high school sport, and becomes an official D1, which we're almost there. So that's where I think the most impactful pickleball engagement would be," she said.

"Our five-year growth plan is to be involved with Major League Pickleball in a big way as well as with pickleball internationally."

She said, "That doesn't mean brick and mortar everywhere, but to help integrate pickleball in all the schools in UAE, Doha and Saudi Arabia. We want to help the Minister of Education and Minister of Sport and bring this out on the basketball court."

She continues, "We'll be doing a pickleball pop-up in Japan at the US Expo for Expo 2025 Osaka. Mega events are a big part of my background, but more importantly, where we feel that sport and brands get elevated the quickest."

Jodi is fascinated with how unique the industry is.

"We can't see each other as competitors right now, whether that's paddle companies or facilities, because the industry is so young."

Says Jodi, "I think that's what's been most impactful for me. Everyone is willing to get on a call. We're learning from each other."

"I think everyone has the same goal of making this sport boom in a healthy way. And obviously I love being a young female in sports cause there's not a lot of representation in the other sports industries. So pickleball has given me that power to really start my own company."

"The real growth behind pickleball is the human connection," says Jodi.

"And I think companies will be really successful and individuals will be really successful if they go more for the human connection rather than the revenue side of things. Obviously, revenue is extremely important for the sport's growth, but if we continue that human connection boom, we'll be unmatchable in any other sport."

Joe Gannascoli
Pickleball Mafia

In the gym one morning for a routine workout, Joe caught part of a conversation.

"These older ladies were talking about wanting to play a pickleball game but being one short," he said.

Feeling bad, Joe decided to jump in.

"I felt bad and figured I could probably handle myself, as I'm athletic, having played baseball and basketball growing up and shifting to paddleball and racquetball as an adult."

So, borrowing a paddle, Joe went to the wall and started hitting against it to warm up.

"They weren't very good, but we still had fun."

Joe never thought it was a game he would want to do.

"I don't want to live in Florida and didn't understand the game."

But soon he found out that it took some skill to play pickleball.

"I wound up liking it and went back the next day to play again."

When Joe started playing pickleball, he often noticed that people wanted to play with someone else.

"When I started, I thought I was better than I was. The games would be a blowout, and I'd hardly get any points."

He continues, "I could always tell from someone's body language. So, I started to work really hard on getting my game to a higher competitive level, and now I can handle myself most of the time, even with the weight."

Knowing a friend at Franklin Sports, Joe asked him to send a paddle.

"I started looking around to see what pickleball was and quickly realized that I needed to get a real paddle."

Since then, Joe has built his collection to nearly eighteen total.

"Every time I like a paddle, I get it. Then I see something else, I try it, and I like it and then I go to another paddle. I think I finally found the paddle that I like and have been using consistently," he said.

"Pickleball is where I really started losing weight and got serious about the science of dieting. It really helped! Right after golf I go play for an hour and a half and then again in the afternoon. All the time, I would be getting a great workout," he said.

"In between those two, I'd eat one meal, maybe a little breakfast, a little banana, and some nuts in the morning. And that's where I lost a hundred pounds. I still have 50 to knock off."

Joe has always been known for being a perfectionist in his trades.

"When I become obsessed with something I want to be good at, really good at it. I'm competitive."

He approached his acting and cooking careers the same way.

"I'm self-taught in everything I do. I watch as many videos as I can. I read and I learned that you have to become good enough to do something without having to think about it. It's gotta be rote. My game is getting there."

Always traveling, Joe's paddles are packed and ready for action.

"I always Google pickleball courts near me. And I play in North Carolina, South Jersey, upstate New York, Florida, wherever I go. There is always a pickleball game to be found."

He continues, "Some of the competition is good, some is not good. But I can always work on shots and take it easy and just play easy games. I love it."

He said, "The first time I traveled without a paddle, I was in North Carolina, and I was watching games and people weren't really saying hello or smiling. Finally, I said, does anybody have a TV here? Has anyone ever seen The Sopranos?"

With that comment, Joe was offered a paddle to play.

"Most of the time someone will notice me, and it makes it easier to get into games."

Unlike acting, Joe tends to be quiet when he plays pickleball.

Joe says, "I'm not a talker. I don't like to talk between shots. I just want to play and am always thinking about the next shot I'll hit. I'm there to play ball, and I want to win. Always."

"Everyone tells me that I look better now than I did when I was on the show. I feel so much better," he said.

One hundred pounds lighter, Joe loves shopping for clothes.

"I just feel so much better and sleep better and can't wait to start the day."

He said, "Maybe I'm not used to running. I had a double hip replacement when I was on The Sopranos, and they needed me. As soon as they killed me on the show, I had double hip replacement done the same day."

Joe can now move better on the court when they try drop shots.

"Sometimes I get to them, sometimes I don't. At 66, I've fallen a few times like everyone, but I don't want too serious an injury and be laid up too long."

On a trip to Boca Raton, Joe's pickleball partner mentioned the theater and told him a friend was doing a show there.

"He goes, 'My wife runs it'. And he turned out to be a comedian and a news producer. We became friends."

Joe continues, "He was giving out cards with upcoming shows and one of them was Office Trivia. I told him we should do one on The Sopranos."

The two collaborated with Joe writing a skit to promote the show.

"It had so many views and people loved it so much that I decided to create a story of why I'm in Boca in this ice cream store."

The team turned that idea into a sizzle reel.

"We hope to turn it into a show and need to shoot the pilot. All this came from a pickleball game."

Off the court, Joe loves conversations.

"No matter what I do, no matter who I meet, I'll always ask them what they do. And I love to take pictures with fans of the show," he said.

Joe also continues to build his other brands.

"I'm a brand ambassador for a vodka company called Rakavaka Vodka and do cooking events in homes and restaurants for Sopranos fans. I love to introduce people to people and help make connections for potential business opportunities."

"I'd love to be testing paddles. I love testing paddles. And I want to sponsor events."

Joe continues to look for ways to support the game of pickleball and build his brands at the same time.

"Maybe I can get involved in some pro-ams, play a little, cook some food, and maybe even win a game or two. I just need to get my skills up a little more first. Maybe get some lessons from a pro."

A travel enthusiast, Joe wants to do anything that has to do with pickleball, with a tour in Sicily planned this October.

"My daughter snickers at me now when I play on our trips. But I hope she gets on the court with me one day, as I see lots of other fathers and daughters do it. There is no barrier to this game," he said.

Just like his character Vito in The Sopranos, Joe's famous line now is, "I'm always looking to earn, have fun, and do what I want to do."

But he does have some pet peeves.

"I play at a place in Florida with four courts. On a weekend you might have to wait 15 minutes for the next game. People need to be more courteous sometimes. Don't sit on the court after a game and talk. The next group is waiting. Sometimes they forget the character I played on TV."

Joy Macci

Joy of Pickleball

Joy says, "Pickleball didn't just find me—it awakened something within me. A calling. A mission. A spark I didn't know I was missing."

A little over six years ago, a dear friend and respected colleague, Craig Bell, former Director of Racquet Sports at Bent Tree Country Club, said, "Joy, you've got to try this game."

She continues, "We had co-authored a tennis book together, and when he told me about this quirky-sounding sport with an even quirkier name, I knew it was worth a swing. From the first few hits, I got hooked immediately!"

Joy loves how the game combines sports she played growing up like ping pong, badminton, and tennis.

"What's so fun about it is the people. It's the only sport for all ages and all levels, where you can bring together the kids, the parents, the grandparents all on one court, with everyone having a wonderful time."

"Pickleball isn't just a game; it's an instant community," says Joy.

"On one court, you'd see three generations—kids, parents, and grandparents ... another court players of all ages, levels, sizes and nationalities, all sharing laughter, high-fives, and fierce rallies. That kind of connection? It's rare. And it's magic."

"I got spoiled early on with paddles ... a USAPA Ambassador kindly let me sample a variety of her paddles, before purchasing one. Then, as my game and coaching progressed, Diadem Sports sponsored me for both their pickleball paddles and tennis racquets," says Joy.

"Diadem produces great products, and I've been honored to use and rep them for years. Plus, I was recently approached by Velvet Athletics to partner and create a signature JOY paddle with them."

She continues, "Our games are always evolving, and it causes players to want to try out new paddles. That's another neat thing about the game."

A couple of months before the US Open Pickleball Championships, a senior doubles team reached out in a panic.

"Joy, we've just received a last-minute wildcard entry to the US Open and quickly need your high-level coaching to get us ready."

"We hit the court immediately—focusing on sharpening strategy, tuning mechanics, and mastering mindset."

"They didn't just want to play. They wanted to become and win."

And they did.

Says Joy, "They didn't just show up—they rose to the moment. They played their hearts out...shocking everyone...walking on with a wildcard entry and walked away as Silver Medalists at one of the sport's most prestigious stages. That's the magic of belief, coaching, and grit—working together in rhythm."

Joy had fun and was honored to serve as anchor broadcaster and sports commentator at the Texas Open Pickleball Championships in Coppell, an unforgettable role where she witnessed the best of the best in action.

"In one iconic match, 13-year-old Anna Leigh Waters and her mom Leigh faced Simone Jardim and Lucy Kovalova in the Women's Pro Gold Medal Finals. The fire, the finesse, the fearlessness—it was unforgettable."

Joy continues, "From the moment I saw her play, I knew Anna Leigh Waters wasn't just a rising star—she was a superstar in the making!"

"My journey has taken me around the world—teaching, coaching, and witnessing the Joy of Pickleball in action," says Joy.

In Mexico, standing on top of beautiful Los Cabos Resort's two brand-new pickleball courts overlooking the ocean with 10 paddles and 12 balls, 28 players of all ages, levels, and nationalities joined her for a two-hour morning pickleball clinic, some holding a paddle for the first time.

She said, "With limited gear and unlimited joy, what began as drills turned into laughter, connection, and friendships that now span countries and united the group into one universal language—the language of sport and pickleball!"

"In the Dominican Republic, where very few knew anything about the sport of pickleball, we turned a local basketball court into a pickleball haven using painter's tape, portable net and passion."

She continues, "In less than five minutes, to see the joy and excitement in their eyes as they hit their first serves and dinks, played their first games while I instructed the local players, coaches, and staff, I realized this sport has us contributing something much greater than ourselves."

"Pickleball is like magic," says Joy.

"It transforms people from the inside out, that's what's uniquely different about the sport. It empowers people. It ignites people. While the game connects people and unites people."

"Pickleball has powerfully and purposefully impacted my life in so many ways," says Joy.

"After 40 years of coaching tennis worldwide, I have worked with world champions, global executives, Olympic medalists, and tennis legends. My client list has included Serena and Venus Williams, Andy Roddick, Jennifer Capriati, Fortune 500 and sports industry executives, celebrities, and Olympians."

She continues, "But it's through pickleball that I've seen people truly transform—physically, emotionally, and spiritually."

"That's why almost seven years ago, I founded and became CEO of Joy of Pickleball, a company that provides world-class coaching, training, and travel to expand and grow the great sport globally," says Joy.

"To be honest, it's been refreshingly fun learning and mastering a new sport and business! I still lovingly teach a little bit of tennis, but a majority of my time and energy is going into growing the sport of pickleball globally."

"I have a full range of students, all ages 3 to 83, from handicapped, local, state, and national champions to certified coaches."

Joy continues, "The sport is still in its infancy and growing very quickly. I love being a part of growing something on a global level, making connections with people, impacting their lives."

Whether it's helping a retiree become a certified coach, mentoring a seventh-degree black belt from 3.5 to 5.0 in six months, or guiding complete beginners through their first dinks, Joy has seen pickleball transform lives time and time again.

"Throughout this journey, I've had the privilege of being a featured speaker at major international gatherings including the World Pickleball Conference, Pickleball Minds, and PickleCon," says Joy.

"Each platform allows an opportunity to share the joy, the science, and the soul of this sport with players, coaches, business leaders, and innovators shaping the next era of pickleball."

In Dubai, Joy was honored to speak at the Pickleball Minds Business Forum, where leaders from more than 30 nations gathered to connect, collaborate, and envision the global future of the sport. It was there she shared a truth that drives her.

"Pickleball is more than a sport. It's soul. It's a spark. It's the fastest-growing connector of people on the planet."

"And recently I was surprised and deeply honored to receive the 2025 Golden Pickle Business Award at the World Pickleball Conference in Palm Beach—recognizing excellence and impact in expanding the sport's global business and community reach," says Joy.

"To be acknowledged not just as a coach or speaker, but as a catalyst in this global pickleball evolution is a responsibility I gratefully carry with purpose and passion."

Back in the U.S., one of Joy's favorite stories and students is a truly remarkable disabled athlete.

"She previously was an elite mountain bike competitor prior to her devastating accident. Physically her left shoulder and immobile left arm, following seven unsuccessful surgeries, needed to be sport taped into the socket before every lesson," says Joy.

"Her usable right paddle hand has the third middle finger cut off at the joint, and emotionally, she deals daily with high-level stress and pressure with a husband who is battling stage 4 cancer. Weekly she and her lifelong best friend come for lessons and all of us experience first-hand the miracle of healing and life transformation as she reconnects with the love, laughter, hope, and joy of pickleball."

"This is what's so exciting about pickleball. It helps heal people. It helps transform people. It also helps us get back a balanced life," says Joy.

"When you're having a tough day or something crazy goes on, you go out and play a couple games of pickleball. Then you can deal with anything."

Joy always enjoys being playful and loves to show it with her Joy of Pickleball clothing.

"To me, what's fun about pickleball is the more colorful, the more people love it because it brings life back into the game. You get someone that's like a 75-year-old lady, who then steps into an outfit that's neon pink and neon yellow or neon green and neon blue. And she feels like she's 25 years old again. That's the power of color, and the power of fun!"

"Pickleball gives us purpose," says Joy.

"We can connect with people, and ourselves. Some people are retired and bored. They don't know what to do, because they've given up that big job that was their identity."

One of her students owned a Tae Kwon Do Studio.

"He's a seventh-degree black belt, who had recently retired and sold his business. I challenged him to reach for greatness in a new sport and a new identity. I coached him up to a 5.0 player from a 3.5 player in six months. Now I'm mentoring him as a certified coach and I'm going to show others how to make this same transformation in their game. Spread the word."

"We're not just building better players—we're building a global community," says Joy.

"And maybe, just maybe, we're paving the way for a future Olympic sport. With the right vision, the right energy, and the power of inclusion, I believe pickleball will be in the Brisbane 2032 Olympics."

That is exactly what pickleball is doing, uniting the world one paddle, one serve, one joyful connection at a time.

"I still love coaching. I still love color (the bolder, the better!). And I still believe that on any given day, with just sneakers and a smile, you can walk up to a pickleball court and be welcomed into a game, and into a community that changes lives. That is the Joy of Pickleball!"

Julie Scott

Order on the Court!

J ulie's introduction to pickleball came through her son, Kyle Yates.

"With a background in ping-pong, he was a natural at the game, which led to his professional career."

She continues, "My story was like many others. I started in a community center, got into the tournament scene and rose to a 4.5 level player. My husband, Larry, and I traveled lots, lost lots, and decided to move over to the referee side of the game."

"Kyle's journey as a pro has been amazing. In my opinion, he's the one who started growing the sport."

"Holding the #1 ranking for over three years, he was about the only young player at the time and the first to get a paddle endorsement (Paddletek). They didn't play for money back then."

Julie knows the sport is still so young.

"Many involved with the referee side of the game are now pressing to get paid more. But we have to be patient and realize that the game has come so far. It takes time to get there, but we will ... one day. Everyone needs to be more patient."

"Refereeing is fun and very social," says Julie.

"You get to be on the court with the best players in the world. To me, it's more fun to referee than to compete. And there is no pressure with the job, only what you put on yourself."

Even after having once been a soccer mom, Julie had never officiated any sports.

Julie said, "In the early days (2016) we would stay with the tournament director at a tournament in Michigan and get paid like $5 a match with coupons for a free lunch."

"That was the early phase of what is now our official referee system."

"It wasn't until around 2018 that USA Pickleball started a tiered referee program, and getting certified became a process," says Julie.

"USA Pickleball's sanctioned events required referees. This is when the referee program really started to take off."

"It was difficult to find enough referees, so the recruiting and training really picked up."

"I think there are over three or four hundred certified referees now," says Julie.

"I'm the referee coordinator for the APP, and I go to most all their tour stops."

At the US Open, she oversaw 127 referees.

"That's the most that I've had to manage."

Even now, Julie still works when not coordinating others.

"I am the Certified Referee Coordinator for the Atlantic South region for USA Pickleball," says Julie.

"I've gone to places like Puerto Rico, St. Thomas, Hawaii and even Ireland where I trained referees and even played in the Irish Open."

"Most recently, my husband and I traveled to Italy and England to train and assess referees for the European Pickleball Federation. I truly enjoy this job."

Julie was also one of 12 referees to officiate the 2024 World Cup in Lima, Peru.

Now traveling extensively, Julie's role as a referee coordinator puts her right in the middle of all the action.

"It wasn't long ago that we had players stay with us at our home," says Julie.

"I can remember walking into my living room and seeing someone I don't know sleeping on the couch. Kyle had invited them back, because they needed a place to stay."

"Kyle mentored and brought in Ben Johns when he was just starting pickleball. He was at Anna Leigh Waters' 12th birthday and gave her a paddle. They both ended up as Kyle's partners in the past."

These days, most of Julie's social circle has switched to referees.

"I'm in charge of the Atlantic South Region, and we now have the largest contingency of credentialed USA Pickleball referees."

Julie credits some of this growth to the Snowbirds.

"There is lots of training here, and lots of interest to learn to referee."

It's still a pay-for-travel model, but Julie is working hard with her organization so that the referees aren't losing money doing their job.

"All of them do this mostly for the friendships, for the camaraderie, and for the fun. We have become a family."

With social media so prevalent, the referees have created their own online groups.

"There's one on Facebook called Pickleball Referees in Training. And that's where we usually post most of the pictures from the tournaments, our group photos or congratulations to someone who moved up one level in the referee training program."

"It has caught on, as now there is a page for each region and also a Certified Referees of USA Pickleball group on Facebook. Additionally, there is also a Facebook page for players who have questions about the rules of pickleball, Ask The Referees."

"We have become so close. One time, we had this trivia game. One of the questions was 'Who once cheered for the University of Kentucky?'"

"Everyone voted for one of the men who looked like he could have done that. But they were wrong. No one knew it was me."

Julie is constantly surprised by who she works with.

"One was a homicide detective, and one of our referees worked for the FBI. They have some interesting backgrounds."

The need for referees is continually growing as the sport continues to grow.

"We're going to need referees for the high school and colleges as competition at this level has begun."

"So, it's a constant effort to actively recruit and train for this need."

Some of the toughest calls are made with the weather conditions.

"It might be fog, it might be rain from the night before, or it might be a storm that's coming," says Julie.

"Our goal is always to give the fans and players a great experience."

At a tournament in Cincinnati, there was a tornado-like storm.

"Right around 4 o'clock we had to suspend play, and it was a good call."

Moments later the tents, the video boards and anything not tied down were blown all over.

"That was crazy. I think we had ten tents destroyed," says Julie.

When asked about the difference between working inside or outdoors, Julie replied, "It's very loud indoors and the spaces are tight, so you have to talk louder. I'm always worried about the players behind me running into me or hitting me with the ball."

"But the upside is we don't have to worry about the weather."

"People just love pickleball. So, it never gets too rowdy, not where we are anyway. We don't let it," says Julie.

"That's one thing about having referees. We want sportsmanship and not drama. If we see that it's going to get out of control, we nip it in the bud ... fast!"

Since adding pickleball to her life, Julie has reconnected with many friends.

"One of my brother's best friends in high school and I ran into him at a tournament in New Orleans with Drew Brees. So, we met and spent a few days together," says Julie.

"And I once posted about being in Cincinnati for a tournament. A cousin I hadn't seen in 25 years saw it, and he and his wife drove from Columbus to say hello."

On an Uber ride, Julie had a discussion with the driver.

"We talked about the name, and why it wouldn't change. When I asked if he played, the driver said, 'No, but I've wanted to.' Everybody is talking about it now."

Pickleball has consumed her family's life.

"My daughter Sarah lives in North Carolina, and she won the gold medal at the 2017 US Open, pairing with Kyle in the mixed doubles."

Now her daughter and husband have a pickleball court in the backyard.

"They are really good friends with a few of the NASCAR drivers who come to their house and play."

Not growing up watching NASCAR, Julie has become a fan.

"Living in North Carolina now, I started watching races and cheering for certain drivers. It's just crazy."

"I am really enjoying what I'm doing right now. We're actually going to go, my husband and I, to Europe next year with three other couples that we have met through pickleball. Just for fun!"

Says Julie, "I love pickleball because it has brought me together with so many people that I would never have been brought together with if it hadn't been for pickleball."

Kaitlin Miller

The Voice of Pickleball

Back in high school, Kaitlin didn't even realize she had played pickleball.

She said, "We had some wooden paddles and were in the gym. It wasn't until COVID that some of my friends got me to play."

Not knowing the game, her mother bought a cheap set of paddles and gave Kaitlin one.

"That's how it all started."

When Kaitlin moved to Nashville, she really started playing.

"I played in a rooftop pickleball tournament at the 505-apartment complex here, which is pretty well known. And that's when I kind of met my mixed doubles partner."

She continues, "They told me I was a natural talent, and really needed to start playing more."

"At the time, my mixed doubles partner and I were playing all these local tournaments and getting first or second in most of them."

Seeing an opportunity to win a lottery, Kaitlin decided to go for it.

"Naples is a really special place to me because my aunt and uncle have a home there. I grew up going there. I was like, wow, that would be a dream to play at the US Open in a place that's very special to me."

The team ended up qualifying in their first event.

Says Kaitlin, "It was also the first year I worked with Pickleball Channel, where I did a lot of broadcasting and storytelling at the US Open. That event was really like a game changer for me, not only as a player, but it also opened my eyes to just how special the community is. It changed my whole pickleball journey."

Broadcasting for the Fox channel (Fox 17 News) in Nashville, Kaitlin did everything she could to incorporate pickleball into TV segments.

"I would do live broadcasts at events, develop partnerships with our local sports teams, and get A-list celebrities involved in the game," says Kaitlin.

Her interviews have included big names like Dustin Lynch, Riley Green, Chase Rice, Zach Top, and other musical artists on tour.

With all her success, Kaitlin was approached by the Pickleball Channel.

"They did a feature on me, so then I helped them out interviewing the pros at clinics during the US Open and all the inspiring stories of the amateurs and volunteers at 'Party in the Park' that happens the first Saturday of tournament week."

Kaitlin interviewed players like Megan Fudge and Ryler Dehart to tell their stories.

"It was so much fun!"

"This past year, I got to do content for both the Pickleball Channel and the U.S. Open," says Kaitlin.

"It's been a great relationship, and they've treated me really well. I love supporting both groups."

Kaitlin is always looking for a great story.

"Last year, we did an awesome series with two three-generation families playing in the US Open. One family was Anna Leigh Waters, her mother and her grandfather."

"They were really a big advocate for this as I quickly became very immersed in the pickleball world here in Nashville."

Kaitlin was soon brought out to Phoenix to be on a show at Pickleball Kingdom.

"It never aired, but it was a great networking experience for national connections."

In Nashville, Kaitlin quickly became a figurehead for the sport.

"All the teams embraced pickleball. The Nashville Sounds had a pickleball night where they gave the first few hundred people into the stadium a free Sounds pickleball paddle."

The team even had an area set up with pickleball courts where fans could play.

After being approached by Nashville Soccer Club's leadership team, Kaitlin was asked to become the face of Summer Fest.

"We put up pickleball courts in the soccer stadium and had a fun event for families," says Kaitlin.

"It was great for our community to see how the sports teams are embracing pickleball."

Kaitlin was also asked to host and participate in the CMA Fest Celebrity Pickleball Tournament.

"They had a pickleball tournament and asked me to MC and play in it. I was Dustin Lynch's partner. Even on tour, musicians like Dierks Bentley and Morgan Evans play. It's been amazing to just see that all unfold."

Kaitlin has been surprised at the popularity of the game at the collegiate level.

"I see a lot of people playing. I was just commentating at the DUPR Collegiate National Championship, doing social media content to show the growth of pickleball. That was very eye-opening for me, as I didn't know how pickleball had grown with this group."

"I've had a lot of the juniors on my podcast, but I was not really familiar with the whole collegiate world," says Kaitlin.

"Speaking with Timber Tucker (the Indiana University coach) I learned that scholarships are now being awarded. I'm fascinated by what this sport is doing for college students, on and off the court."

"What's unique about it is they're allowing grad school students to also compete for the club team and travel. And they're really trying to get more women involved on that level," says Kaitlin.

Working with Pickleball Kingdom as a coach, the club now hosts 'single and mingle' events with open play to attract more young players.

Kaitlin is not surprised with the growth of the game.

"It's a great hobby and outlet for all ages."

She continues, "It's an easy sport to pick up. You can go to most any park and start playing."

Now working for Court Kings, Kaitlin met one of the owners on the pickleball court.

"We were playing pickleball at Lifetime, and he knew about my current involvement with the game."

Following Kaitlin on Instagram, the company was impressed with her success.

"He loved that I was entrepreneurial with projects like my podcast."

Over a cup of coffee, Kaitlin thought the two were just going to discuss the pickleball industry and share advice.

"Much to my surprise, he wanted to hire me to help grow their business."

Starting out part time, as she still had a role with Fox, Kaitlin quickly realized this could be a new professional path.

"My TV contract was up January of 2025," says Kaitlin.

After nine years in the industry, climbing the ladder in a major market, she decided to give it all up and transition all of her efforts to pickleball.

"It was scary to make a shift, but it's been amazing."

Kaitlin has been able to stay in front of the camera with broadcasting projects.

Kaitlin loves how her worlds collided.

"It's become the best of both worlds as I can compete, still be in journalism, and now represent an amazing company in the industry."

Since getting into pickleball, Kaitlin has reconnected with many people.

"My family has a place on Long Beach Island, New Jersey and I go back every summer."

Growing up as an ocean lifeguard in the summers, the island now has a huge pickleball scene.

Says Kaitlin, "I've reconnected with so many people there. I also have friends from North Carolina reaching out who comment on my journey. It's been so awesome."

"I'm a huge fan of open play, and think it's one of the coolest things," says Kaitlin.

"It really is a nice break those two hours you're on the court. You are present, mingling, meeting new people."

Traveling often, Kaitlin keeps a pickleball paddle in her luggage.

"I'll show up to an open play by myself and meet people I never thought I would and some of them lead to really good connections and some new friendships. Never before would I just show up alone to play a sport."

Kaitlin has become close with many of the owners, players, referees and volunteers now at the U.S. Open.

"We literally have a reunion every year in Naples, Florida. And they've connected me with so many great people. It's become my favorite annual tradition."

With an eye for a story, Kaitlin shares a favorite.

"There was this guy in Florida named Petey Bruce who was living in a van. One day, he showed up at a pickleball court," says Kaitlin.

"Missing both his legs and only one arm, he didn't even have prosthetic limbs because he couldn't afford them."

Invited onto the court, he winced in pain but immediately loved the game.

"He figured out a way to strap the paddle on both nubs and started playing, immediately becoming immersed in the pickleball community."

Kaitlin continues, "The local pickleball community took him in, helped him get his prosthetic limbs, find work, and most importantly find a home. It saved his life."

Kaitlin had Petey on her podcast, *Kitchen Talk: Pickleball Edition*, and then later featured him on the news.

"Turns out he's getting a prosthetic leg from an organization in Nashville."

Working with player Stephanie Lane, they arranged a feature on her backyard court.

"His name is Petey Bruce, and we went with him on his prosthetic leg appointment. It was eye-opening!"

"I was in tears when he said how the pickleball community had saved his life," says Kaitlin.

"Now he has a place to live. He has legs where he can play sports and not be in pain. I'm hoping to see him at the U.S. Open."

She continues, "It's moments like this I'll never forget. There will never be any moment or any medal more special."

So how many of the general public know anything about pickleball?

Says Kaitlin, "Evan Slaughter and I went to Broadway in Nashville holding posters of Anna Leigh Waters and Ben Johns asking people if they knew either. Maybe 10% did."

She continues, "It's been great to see the sport start taking off. We are still young, but the numbers show that more people are starting to follow pickleball."

"I really wonder if people will watch the game on TV. For me, I believe the sport is very niche and will be driven by both amateur play and the pros," says Kaitlin.

"Social media continues to be a powerful tool for viewers. Especially with influencers taking more interest in the game."

Kaitlin knows that there are many untold stories of the pickleball communities.

"There are so many cool stories out there that people really aren't hearing. And I wanted to give a voice to that through social media."

She continues, "Keeping it inspiring, lighthearted, interesting, that's really where the content is. And that's kind of the takeaway I've gotten at this point."

She's even started her own podcast called *Kitchen Talk: The Pickleball Edition.*

"Here I share untold stories of pickleball players, businesses and community leaders on a global scale."

Working off hours in the news industry, Kaitlin is so thankful for pickleball.

"I literally have moved everywhere not knowing a single soul. I was just going after that dream to make it to a number one TV market. It was very hard to do that and very isolating."

She continues, "Thank God I met these people at like 8 to 10 a.m. that played pickleball. I got my interaction, I got my workout, my training and I met new people."

Having had two back surgeries after a college career in crew at UCLA, Kaitlin never thought she would compete at a high level again.

"Pickleball has given me a chance to work hard at something, have goals, play at the 5.0 level, win medals and just keep getting better and better while having a great support system of players that also want to do the same."

"At my birthday party, it was a pickleball event and I had like 30 people show up for me, like my closest friends in Nashville. Pickleball has become most of my life in so many different capacities."

Kaitlin continues, "The court's great and it's helped me physically, but off the court, having these opportunities to compete at a US Open and go back to a place that's so important to my family, I feel the sky's the limit."

Kaitlin wants to become a pioneer in this sport.

"I want to elevate myself and my brand in a lot of ways other than just actually stepping foot on the court. That's what I love about pickleball."

"I want to grow youth pickleball on a global scale," says Kaitlin.

She volunteers at schools to teach underprivileged children how to play the sport.

"It's so affordable and accessible, because all the school needs is a gym floor or parking lot, a few nets and cheap paddles."

She continues, "It's been so amazing to see children who never played a sport hit a ball for the first time. Their smile lights up the whole room."

That's why Kaitlin had people bring paddles for her birthday party so they could be donated.

"I'd like to see pickleball grow in elementary, middle, high schools, colleges and beyond."

Kamryn Blackwood

From DUPR Girl to Broadcaster on PBTV

"I was living in LA when the pandemic hit. Like a lot of people, I chose to leave a big city and moved back to New Mexico because everything shut down," says Kamryn.

"My old tennis coach asked if I would coach tennis and pickleball?"

With no other way to make money, Kamryn agreed to tennis but not pickleball.

Back in familiar surroundings, she got back on the court.

"I didn't want to learn something new, and pickleball seemed lame since I was only seeing grandparents playing the sport at the time."

Her coach was OK with it and took all those lessons himself.

"He started making way more money than me and started getting booked out all the time. Here I was on the tennis court not really enjoying myself at all because I was so burnt out from playing collegiately, I almost wanted no part of it anymore."

"I decided to try and figure this whole pickleball thing out."

Her former coach and business partner, Jeremy, taught Kamryn the game.

"He's been super close to me in my life, especially on the court. His knowledge and expertise helped get me my tennis scholarship, so I trusted him in that process of learning what the game of pickleball was."

Soon, Kamryn was ready to enter a tournament, still not fully understanding the complexity of the game and what competition would actually look like.

"I got overly confident and got beat on pretty bad by a bunch of 60- and 70-year-olds. That humbled me quickly."

Almost breaking her paddle, Kamryn was done.

"I was like, this is the dumbest game ever invented. It's just not for me."

"After that tournament in New Mexico, I had some really important people take me under their wing," says Kamryn.

She retooled her game, making it work for pickleball.

"There were a lot of pros and cons that came with that. On one hand I really started to understand the slower pace and patience up at the kitchen line but almost lost a lot of my strengths throughout the process. I listened a little too closely to what 'pickleball' was to the older generation I was currently playing versus the younger competition I was going to be competing against, where I needed my big drives, fast movement and power as well."

Entering a pro tournament in Dallas, Kamryn was matched with Lea Jansen.

"I got wiped off the court and felt like her warm-up."

In mixed doubles it wasn't much better.

"We went up against Anna Leigh Waters and J.W. Johnson losing that match as quickly as my first one."

Says Kamryn, "As hard as those first round losses were, it was still pretty cool to see the game from this perspective. The faster pace, younger players and snagging some wins in the back draw gave me confidence that I could have a place in this sport."

"After the tournament, I was home talking with my dad."

Discussing her results and ability to continue to compete, Kamryn knew there was a huge gap with the lack of women marketing pickleball.

"I went on social media, and no females had the presence of a Ben Johns. That's what interested me the most."

Kamryn knew she didn't need to be number one in the world; she could make a name for herself in other ways.

"I saw the positive impact of the game and what it did in my life, and knew I had to be at the forefront of the global expansion of pickleball."

"I started contacting anyone and everyone in the game just to say, do you need a partner? Do you need this? What do you need?"

Kamryn credits Lee Whitewell.

"She's the first person who called me and said, 'Hey, there's a DUPR (new rating system) commercial. Would you like to be in it? We'll fly you to Texas. We'll do the whole bit. Are you interested?'"

That one commercial changed Kamryn's life.

"I was known as the DUPR girl. It sounds silly, but I was very comfortable in front of the camera, and everyone saw it."

After that experience, Kamryn thought maybe she wasn't supposed to be a top player, but somewhere else in the sport.

"Balance was a huge component from the beginning between the camera and my time on the court," says Kamryn.

"When I started looking for a doubles partner, I called Lee again and she introduced me to Parris Todd. Little did I know we would not only play together but also become best friends. I love that girl."

Kamryn was busy playing tons of tournaments.

"In 2022, MLP (Major League Pickleball) was starting its first big expansion with adding more teams and players from around the world. I was training on a court in Albuquerque and got a text from Brooks Wiley (the Commissioner)."

She continues, "I was expecting an offer to join a team, but instead he asked me to be part of the broadcast. My heart sank."

"The news hit me in a weird way because I wanted to be on a team. It took a minute to consider the opportunity."

Kamryn continued, "I told him I didn't know anything about being on camera other than I had been in the USA pageant and a couple of other things."

Kamryn thought to herself what her goal was from the very beginning?

"I have always wanted to spread the word of the game, to be a light in this space, and to bring people into this amazing community."

She decided right then to make the decision to help the MLP by being on camera and said yes.

"Even if someone paid me, I don't think I could ever watch my first interview on court because it's so horrific," says Kamryn.

"But then I really got to learn the business and how to relate to the players on a personal level because I was one myself."

She continues, "I could really get a lot out of them because I was on their side of things and I didn't want to expose them, harm them or trick them into something in an interview."

Her career started off doing the sidelines with MLP, and soon she became the face and loved it.

Says Kamryn, "Then the PPA called. Hannah Johns told me she was doing too much and needed to take a step back. I was offered her spot and took it."

For a while, Kamryn played double duty, often playing until she got out of the pro draw, then throwing on eyelashes before going to broadcast.

"I did that many times till I realized I'm not in my teens anymore and decided to go full-time in broadcasting."

Not long after this decision, the Tennis Channel created Pickleball TV.

"Matt Manasse and I got the phone call asking to co-host the show. I literally had no idea what they meant."

After some clarification, Kamryn called Matt, and they decided to take the job.

"We didn't know why they chose us, except that we both knew the sport and many of the players."

"It was quite an adventure, as neither of us had been on camera like this before," says Kamryn.

"Since then, we have been arm and arm to bring this amazing sport to our national viewers. We work hard to keep the show going, telling stupid jokes and having a blast with the show every week."

As things evolved, Kamryn decided to move to Atlanta.

"She loves her city but has taken on the adventure of flying to LA every week to film Pickleball TV."

"Navigating the travel has been a very big adjustment. Being from the smallest town in New Mexico, we only had one airport. Now I feel like a travel expert. It's so bizarre, but I love it."

"I love pickleball because it gave me friendships for a lifetime. It gave me a new perspective on what hard work actually is and what it means," says Kamryn.

"Now on TV, I think this is the most I've learned in my life. Things like how to communicate through a screen to thousands of people with three other people, producers and everyone in my ear talking to me."

Kamryn knows she'll never be able to show how much gratitude she has for the sport, and the trajectory it has taken her life on.

"I hated tennis after a while, and don't ever want to hate pickleball. I think it's good to keep a balanced life. It's not who I am. It's what I do. And it's helped me stay levelheaded in a sport that changes every minute of every day."

"Pickleball is a sport anyone can play, and anyone can relate to," says Kamryn.

"A grandson can play with his grandfather. One part of the country can play with another. The game is inclusive, not exclusive."

She continues, "Ryan Sherry said it best on tour, relating how a guy in a Ferrari can show up next to a guy on a bicycle and play for three hours."

The game continues to be relatable to all.

Says Kamryn, "You see Ben Johns hit an ATP, and it's something a seven and seventy-year-old can do. But they can't dunk, kick a penalty shot, or throw a touchdown. So, when they hit a shot a pickleball pro can, it makes them feel they are part of the game."

"I always want to give so much gratitude to the older generation. We owe them so much for bringing us into the sport. None of us would be here if our grandparents had never invited us to play."

Kamryn's family is always reaching out about pickleball.

"Out of the blue, a cousin from Utah calls. We hadn't talked in like eight years, and he wanted to know if a rule was legit."

She continues, "My whole family will call me all the time and say, 'Did you see that they just split up? Did you see this?' And I'm like, yeah, I'm reporting. I see it probably quicker than anyone in this sport, but I get it all the time. And it's great. I love it."

"One of my favorite pickleball stories involves the 'Break the Love Campaign'," says Kamryn.

"We partnered with Walmart in Dallas, brought in over 500 kids, and had a massive event with pickleball and tennis."

Kamryn is also proud of how the industry remains supportive.

"You can call up companies like Franklin, Joola or Selkirk, ask them to donate some equipment, and they will send hundreds of paddles."

She continues, "And celebrities are the same way. You can reach out to them, and they always say yes. It doesn't have that uppity feeling that you get with some golf and tennis events."

"I really do love hosting events," says Kamryn.

"I feel like Matt (Manasse) and I are like the boy and girl version of each other. We love to kind of fly around and do fun events like that."

From the start, Kamryn has been appreciative of how players get paid.

"It's been equal pay from the beginning, and I credit that to Anna Leigh Waters. She has become the female face of the sport, and I would go as far to say the face of the sport right now. She helped us solidify the equal pay discussion from the beginning and put pickleball in the professional realm amongst the most popular sports we see on TV."

As the sport continues its journey, Kamryn knows that adjustments still have to be made.

"It's hard to put that small little court in a stadium of 20,000. It doesn't translate well like tennis does."

She continues, "I always say give tennis singles, let us keep doubles."

"I think pickleball tournaments are getting better," says Kamryn.

"They just mic'd up the benches the past two tournaments. It was really cool to see Julie Johnson and Leigh Waters coach their kids and have completely different patterns and game plans that they wanted them to execute."

Kamryn is now also involved with a new pickleball clothing company.

"There are a lot of them, but I'm really invested in this one called M U E V," says Kamryn.

"I'm really passionate about it. They're listening to my ideas and we're changing things."

"I didn't think in one year I would be hosting a show on the Tennis Channel," says Kamryn.

"I still laugh about it because I didn't even know the industry when I started. I have so much more to learn but am so excited for what lies ahead."

Kelli Alldredge
Chicken and Pickle

Once a competitive tennis player, Kelli Alldredge was first introduced to pickleball in 2016.

"One of my tennis buddies was friends with Dave Johnson, the Founder of Chicken N Pickle, and invited me to play pickleball with them one weekend. I'd never heard of it, but it sounded fun, and I agreed to hop on a court."

Kelli fell in love with pickleball, and began playing regularly at Chicken N Pickle, where she got to know Dave.

"He would occasionally play with us and our interactions on the court spurred this journey for me."

Starting her career at Chicken N Pickle as the director of community impact in 2018, Kelli was named President in 2023. Each location has between eight and fourteen courts, with expansive dining spaces, game yards for family-friendly fun and rooftops for hosting birthday parties, corporate events and community fundraisers.

"Our courts are always full, and for that, we are so blessed," says Kelli.

"The majority of our customers come with family or friends to eat, drink and hang out; many are not there for pickleball, which comprises about 20% of our business. But it's always our goal to get paddles in hands because we believe once you get on the court, you'll be hooked!"

Though overseeing the company's efforts in the pickleball space is an important part of her role, identifying ways to positively impact the company's communities is paramount.

One of Chicken N Pickle's key differentiators is its commitment to community. Every location employs a full-time Community Impact Coordinator and it's their job to do something to serve their community every day of the year.

"We've hosted thousands of events across our properties, from cornhole tournaments and family bingo, to providing a space for nonprofit boards to meet and families of terminally ill children to gather so they can make memories together over a meal. Our footprint is large, and we consider it a blessing to have space that allows us to give back in so many ways - we love using our properties for good."

Chicken N Pickle gives back daily to support the local community, and though many of those efforts involve pickleball, there are dozens of ways they give back to non-profits, schools, healthcare organizations and more.

"Proceeds from every non-alcoholic beverage served in a CNP 'community cup' benefit a local charitable organization 362 days a year. And, every Tuesday, all 13 locations host a 10% back night," says Kelli.

"One night in North Kansas City, our 10% back night raised enough to purchase an adaptive bike for an 8-year-old who couldn't ride a traditional bike. There wasn't a dry eye in the house when the new bike was revealed!"

Additionally, one day a year in early September, all Chicken N Pickle locations close their doors for the company's annual "Our hearts are local" day.

"It's my favorite day of the year because our teams spend the morning serving the communities, then reconvene to have lunch and a company-wide pickleball tournament. There is a lot of friendly competition, especially between our front-of-the-house and back-of-the-house team members."

Chicken N Pickle is proud of its commitment to inclusivity and efforts to identify ways for everyone who walks onto the property to have an opportunity to enjoy the sport.

"I'm really proud of our para-pickleball programming," says Kelli.

"All locations offer these clinics twice a month, and two sports chairs made specifically for pickleball are available at each venue, courtesy of The Chicken N Pickle Foundation."

In her time as President, Kelli has seen the program grow tremendously, with some participants driving many hours to attend.

"The success of the program has been humbling. It is not unusual for someone to drive two or three hours to attend," said Kelli.

"These efforts are led by our team member, Taylor Nichols, who is an accomplished para-athlete. He travels to each location when para-pickleball is launched and has inspired so many. When guests see someone who looks like them on the courts, they realize anything is possible. We're happy to play a role in facilitating that inclusive spirit."

In addition to programs for players with physical disabilities, Kelli is also proud of her teams' efforts to serve the autism community. She recalls speaking with a mother who took her child with autism to a public court where they were not invited to play.

"After that experience, she heard about our autism awareness night and after visiting, she raved about how she and her child felt welcomed and could play pickleball without judgment," says Kelli.

"Our team has done a lot of research on how to best host experiences for guests with autism. We've experimented with lighting, different balls, softer music, shorter court reservation times and more. We've also hosted blind and deaf pickleball leagues and the camaraderie on our courts during those events is unmatched."

"I fiercely believe pickleball is for everyone and we love introducing the sport to people who thought they could never play."

Kelli continues, "It's what really motivates us as a company, and we love seeing others on our property get into spirit by cheering for those on the court. We take seriously our role in supporting and uplifting others!"

As the sport of pickleball grew, so did Chicken N Pickle's interest in connecting with players from across the country. Enter the Chicken N Pickle's Ambassador Program. Since 2021, Chicken N Pickle has selected ambassadors from each location who serve as brand advocates while getting to play the sport they love.

"Our ambassador program is application-based and helps us celebrate our most loyal players," says Kelli.

"They not only play a lot of pickleball, but also volunteer heavily in the community, so to have them wearing our gear when they travel for tournaments and advocate for us, it's helped make Chicken N Pickle feel like more than just a pickleball facility."

Kelli has loved introducing her family to pickleball, many of whom shared her original love for tennis.

"It's been really fun to see my children and my parents on the courts! Not long after I began working at Chicken N Pickle, my parents built a court at their lake house for anyone in the neighborhood to enjoy. I love the small-town vibe and energy that the court creates. Every time I pull up, I have no idea who's out there playing, and I love that!"

Kelli's mom, who is seventy-three, plays three times a week at her local Chicken N Pickle and her closest friends have come from the pickleball court.

"Our ladies' community is amazing," says Kelli.

"Our mixers almost always sell out because they're players who love the game, enjoy being competitive and want to continue the camaraderie by heading over to the restaurant to have lunch together. It's more than just a game."

"I don't think people realize what a workout pickleball is," says Kelli.

"They envision someone holding a paddle and standing there to hit the ball. What they don't realize is how much you move up and back on the court, and before you know it, two hours have passed, and you got a great workout."

Kelli laughs as she recalls getting pulled onto the court for a match wearing a sweater and jeans.

"I decided I'd play for a few minutes, but before I knew it, it'd been an hour, and I was still playing in my jeans. I would not go to a gym and lift weights for an hour in my jeans. No way. It'd be miserable."

Chicken N Pickle has 13 locations in Missouri, Kansas, Texas, Oklahoma, Arizona, Nevada and Colorado. Alldredge says the goal is to continue expansion throughout the country, with special emphasis on the Denver, Phoenix and Houston markets. As the company grows, the question remains: what is Chicken N Pickle?

"We talk about this a lot," says Kelli.

"Are we a restaurant? Are we an entertainment venue? Are we a pickleball facility? We are so unique that we fit into none of those categories, and yet we fit in all of them!"

"No matter the category, there's always an emphasis on human connection at Chicken N Pickle."

She continues, "Wherever you are on our property – a pickleball court, the dining room, or up on our rooftop playing cornhole, we are trying to foster human connection by setting down technology and connecting with each other. We want to create this old school vibe that's low tech, high touch and the coolest backyard you never want to leave!"

And, despite having nine years under their belt, Kelli admits the company's leadership team is still learning.

"We pivot often, and I think that humility has done us well. There's a lot we still need to learn, but I'm proud of the efforts that have gotten us this far. There's no guide for how to operate a multi-unit pickleball/restaurant concept so to have the opportunity to chart our own course, it's both exciting and humbling."

"I love pickleball because it changed my life," says Kelli.

"Having an opportunity to work with a growing brand that prioritizes doing good – it doesn't get better than that! Five years from now, I hope I'm sitting in a new Chicken N Pickle seeing the sport continue to grow."

Lieve Olivera
A "Special" Game

"For many years, I was an avid tennis player," says Lieve. "One day, on my way to work out at the gym, I saw people hit a little wiffle ball back and forth, and I thought it looked like a fun game. Shortly after, I decided to try playing pickleball. I was hooked immediately. Now I play three to four times weekly. Initially, pickleball was perceived as a game for older people, but it has evolved rapidly. The game is played at any age, from young children to teens to seniors."

"Due to my background in sport, I was invited to be a Global Ambassador for the International Pickleball Federation," Lieve continues.

As a board member of the International Gymnastics Hall of Fame, she maintains a busy travel schedule.

"As a Global Ambassador, I promote pickleball worldwide, particularly amongst tennis players. It's great to see how Andre Agassi has become an avid pickleball player, and more and more tennis players are joining the game."

While on a trip to Cabo San Lucas for a meeting with the International Gymnastics Hall of Fame, Lieve encouraged her fellow board members to play pickleball.

"I played with my good friend, Olympic Gold Medalist Nadia Comaneci, and several other Olympians who had recently learned about the game. We all had fun! Pickleball truly brings people together, and many new relationships are established."

Lieve continues: "Presently, I'm involved with the Special Olympics Pickleball program. In 2015, I was volunteering for the sport of gymnastics and tennis at the Special Olympics World Games in Los Angeles."

Returning to Florida, Lieve would often pass the local Special Olympics offices in Venice on her way to a pickleball game.

"Every time I passed by, I kept thinking how I could introduce the sport of pickleball to Special Olympics athletes in Florida."

Lieve wrote a letter to the local Director.

"I didn't get a response immediately, so I wrote another letter."

Eventually, she decided to stop by the office to convince the Director in person and hasn't looked back.

"The Director thanked me for sending the letters and informed me that they were waiting for permission from headquarters. A few days later, I was given the go-ahead," says Lieve.

Together with the Director, they decided to convert the basketball court, which was filled with fitness equipment.

"We had to push everything aside to make room for a court, buy the net and balls, and tape the court."

Shortly after, 24 athletes participated in the inaugural Sarasota pickleball season.

"All of our athletes are intellectually challenged. Many are autistic, some have Down Syndrome, and several are severely challenged both physically and intellectually."

She continues, "I had no program, no guidelines, and I simply gathered a few volunteers. I had to be very creative, but we persevered, and it resulted in an immensely successful initial season."

Three months later, the group was invited to the Special Olympics Florida State Classic event at Wide World of Sports in Orlando for an exhibition match.

"It was a wonderful event. That was about six years ago. Presently, I have gathered ten fantastic pickleball volunteers," says Lieve.

"Pickleball has now become part of Special Olympics nationwide. Since then, I've had countless heartwarming experiences with the athletes. The program runs two hours a week for three months. Ages range from 16 to 65, and during each session, we focus on the individual needs of the athlete. Some are mute, some are legally blind, some are deaf, and each athlete is intellectually challenged, several with additional physical challenges."

"Recently, I taught a young man named Kevin," says Lieve.

"He was legally blind and could only utter a few words. For the first few weeks, he did not speak at all. Kevin could barely hold a paddle."

She continues, "We would place a paddle in his hands, and put the ball on top of it. Next, we helped him hit the ball over the net. He loved it. He would smile but not speak! However, one day, he refused to play and sat on the sideline. No matter what I tried, he did not want to play until suddenly I saw him picking up a black paddle, and he joined in. I quickly realized that he only wanted to play with this particular black paddle."

"After Kevin left, I grabbed the black paddle and put it in my bag. The following week, when Kevin walked in, I pulled out the paddle and handed it to him. I'll never forget the smile on his face. He was so happy. That same day, when the session ended, Kevin gave me the biggest bear hug," says Lieve.

"Then he uttered, 'I love you, coach.' I don't have the words to convey what a special moment that was. I was speechless. To see his happiness and hear those words was something I'll never forget. Tears were flowing when I drove home that day."

"Sometimes, we ask our Special Olympics athletes to help each other," says Lieve.

"The way they relate to each other is truly inspiring. I remember when an athlete joined us who was mute."

She continues, "How his fellow athletes communicated with him was beautiful. I was teaching a very simple skill and saw out of the corner of my eye that one of our athletes was communicating in sign language so the student could understand what was being taught."

Last year, Lieve took a mixed doubles team to the Florida state competition.

"It was a very good team, and they made it to the finals. The team eventually lost a close game, and our athletes were dejected and, tearfully and quite loudly, conveyed their disappointment. I realized quickly that I needed to show them that their 'loss' was truly a 'win,' from an angle they could understand."

"I told them they had won a silver medal and had made it to the finals, which was another win, and that they had played the best they could, and that is a win!" says Lieve.

"Both agreed they played their best and that they should be proud of the effort. And I reminded them that this was a game they loved, and that in itself was a win, too."

The life lesson was immediately learned.

"I could visibly see their faces change and understand what winning was all about," says Lieve.

"Afterwards, they proudly walked around showing off their medals to everyone, hugging their family, and their opponents, telling them that they had 'won' a silver medal! Realizing the essence of what 'winning' truly means was such a great turnaround."

"Special Olympics continues to expand the sport nationwide. It's wonderful," says Lieve.

"More and more athletes want to take part in our pickleball program. I used to teach elite gymnastics and judge at world championships and several gymnastics Olympic trials. I have judged around the world. I've truly seen and done it all. I've even given a perfect 10 to the perfect gymnast," says Lieve.

"But when I watch the Special Olympic athletes play pickleball, I see perfection redefined. To me, they define the essence of the sport. They display outstanding sportsmanship, teamwork, joy, and enthusiasm."

So, what effect has pickleball had on Lieve?

"Working with Special Olympic athletes helped me learn more about myself. I always tell my volunteers: 'You are going to spend two hours, and it's all about them, it's not about you. You must forget 'you,' and dedicate every thought, every moment to the athletes, even if a skill requires hundreds of repetitions. You are there for them.'"

"When I started volunteering, I believed that I was teaching the athletes, but the reverse is true; they never fail to teach me!"

Lieve continues, "The joy I experience is indescribable. When they manage to hit a ball over the net, they are happy. They smile. And I smile ... with immense gratitude."

"Helping Special Olympic athletes play pickleball has been one of the greatest gifts I have received in my life."

Marianne Orr

Champion of the Chair

"It's been twenty-eight years since being paralyzed in a car accident," says Marianne.

"Eleven years after my injury and thinking my days of playing sports were over, someone showed up on my doorstep with a flyer for wheelchair tennis."

She quickly embraced the sport and started to travel to competitions.

"It's actually where I met my husband. He was an instructor at the first wheelchair tennis camp I went to."

Eight years after meeting, the two got married.

"My husband had the same level spinal cord injury as me and was also in a chair. We were both fully functional and independent. One month after we got married, he had a stroke. That was a game-changer. I put my life on hold to help care for him."

Marianne was by her husband's side for the next seven years providing continuous care and support.

"It took a lot of my energy. Nevertheless, I was able to participate occasionally in tennis and continued to run both junior and adult wheelchair tennis programs."

"It's been almost two years since his passing. I was lost and had to figure out how to be me again."

With no clear direction, one of her friends invited Marianne to play pickleball.

"At first, I was unsure about it, being a tennis player."

But her friend persisted and got Marianne out on the court.

"This was the beginning of '24, and I started playing for fun. Not long after that, he asked me to be his doubles partner in the U.S. Open that was coming up."

New to the sport, Marianne politely declined. This time.

"He came back from the U.S. Open and asked me what it would take to be his partner in the next event. He told me it would be in August and held in Colorado Springs. So, I said yes."

Playing in her first tournament, Marianne had no expectations.

"I was the only female competing against all males. I played singles, doubles and hybrid."

She ended up winning the gold in singles and bronze in doubles.

"I surprised myself and a lot of the other competitors, too, since I was so new to the sport."

Marianne got back the thrill of competition, meeting new people, developing friendships, and traveling again.

"The world of adaptive sports is a great community. It gave me that little bug and spirit again."

"About a month later, one of the guys who was an Ambassador for USA Wheelchair Pickleball called and talked me into coming to Cincinnati for a tournament," says Marianne.

"Some of the really good players were there and it was fun to play with them. I even surprised myself again and won a silver medal in singles."

With her recent success, Marianne started looking towards Nationals.

"When this all started, it wasn't even in my realm of thinking."

She continues, "However, this was the first time they were going to hold a wheelchair division at Nationals. So that was huge for us to be able to compete on a big stage like that."

"An event the size and scope of Nationals is more about promoting the sport. It shows everyone that wheelchair athletes can be just as competitive as able-bodied, and it's a sport for everyone."

With a stage like this, she jumped at the opportunity to compete.

Marianne had no expectations, other than to support wheelchair pickleball and get the word out.

"It was phenomenal playing at Nationals. I had fun competing at a high level and meeting everyone. It was a great experience."

Being only one of two female wheelchair players there, once again, she competed against all men.

"Onlookers often thought of me as the underdog, and I started to gain a cheering section that followed me from court to court. It was so fun to have people I'd never met cheering me on."

One couple who joined the bandwagon had a daughter in a wheelchair living in New York.

"Their daughter had just started playing pickleball, and they were happy to make a connection for her to the game."

Marianne says, "Pickleball got me moving, competing, and meeting people—it reminded me there's still lots to enjoy in life."

"I'm pretty competitive by nature. One game I played, not long after I first started, my opponent thought he'd have some fun and kick my butt in singles. I beat him every game. I think he was surprised how quickly I was able to pick up the sport."

Transitioning from tennis, Marianne has found it a bit easier to pick up.

"I still have a long way to go and didn't know what I was doing then, but it was fun to be back on a court and competitive again. In fact, I am often the only wheelchair player out there with the able-bodied players."

Marianne loves the social nature of pickleball.

"You can show up at the park and stick your paddle up and play with anybody, which is nice. Whether you are able-bodied, disabled, whatever, it doesn't matter your abilities or skill level. You can just jump in and play. The social part of this game has been huge for me."

"Since my husband's passing a couple of years ago, pickleball has reconnected me with the guy I'm currently dating."

She is part of a group of wheelchair players that get together on Wednesday nights.

"He started playing pickleball with our group last fall. After dating for several months, I showed up to the courts one morning to a surprise proposal with 'Will U Marry Me?' written in two hundred pickleballs spread out across the court. I said 'YES!' and we plan to get married soon. I am so grateful pickleball brought love back into my life. It truly has been wonderful!"

Exciting growth is being experienced on the adaptive side for pickleball.

"More people are learning about the sport and starting to play, which is great," says Marianne.

"At the Open this last year, around twenty-four players competed in the wheelchair division."

"I have seen a lot of players come from other sports. Some have shoulder issues, and pickleball is a little easier on them than sports like basketball or tennis."

"Pickleball has made it easy to make new friends. Everyone loves to get on the courts to play and socialize. We sometimes hold parties at the club. One night we brought in extra sports chairs and threw some of the pros and able-bodied players in them. It was fun watching them try to maneuver the chair and get to the ball. Those who participated gained a new appreciation for the challenges involved in playing in a chair."

Marianne hopes more clubs will offer this.

"I only know a few wheelchair athletes playing at a club. Right now, our group plays at the rec center on a gym floor with portable nets."

Her hope is that clubs start partnering to have sports chairs available for use.

Two months after Marianne competed at Nationals she got a call.

"It was the mom of a junior player I had coached. She congratulated me for being a cover girl. I had no idea what she was talking about, as I had never modeled. I found out that I was on the cover of *Sports and Spokes* magazine, highlighting a pickleball first, the inaugural wheelchair pickleball debut at Nationals. I was honored to be on the cover and interviewed for the article within the magazine."

Growing up, Marianne's family played lots of games.

"We used to play badminton, nine square and volleyball in the backyard. But for New Year's Eve this year, we ended up getting on a pickleball court. Many of my family had never played before. We had a blast!"

"I enjoy pickleball because it's fun, active, and social. It welcomes all ages and abilities. It has helped me connect with others and has given me a life again. I love it!"

Martina Kochli

American Pickleball

Always on the move from base to base, Martina and her husband soon landed in Colorado Springs as her husband served at the 10th Special Forces Group.

"For three years, friends asked me to play pickleball. But I was a collegiate tennis player, and always said no," says Martina.

"But finally, I decided to give it a try."

"Because we never stayed anywhere long, it was hard to keep a job and maintain a healthy network of friends. So, I jumped into pickleball to expand that group."

Not expecting to like the game, the exact opposite happened.

Says Martina, "I jumped in with all my force and decided to play pro pickleball."

The industry was still in its infancy in late 2018.

"I easily connected with top pickleball brands and started traveling and playing professional tournaments. It was really exciting," says Martina.

"There was absolutely no pickleball on military bases, so I found a park downtown that had pickleball."

Martina continues, "It was very unorganized, but the courts were beautiful. And it was absolutely full and hard to get a court."

While teaching at Fisher Island, Miami, one of my clients approached me and said, "You should create 'American Pickleball'."

He proceeds with, "Your husband is serving our country, and you're the professional pickleball player, what could be more fitting?"

That moment sparked the idea, and it was from that conversation that American Pickleball was born; an initiative inspired by service, sport, and the spirit of community.

The couple created a boutique event company and started running pickleball tournaments in Florida.

"Our heart is with the Green Beret Foundation. So, this was sort of us bringing attention to the military and focusing on special forces."

Martina continues, "It's great for families as the soldiers redeploy, as anyone can play."

"Pickleball is a great opportunity for someone to play a sport where you really can just jump in, pick up a paddle and go play. Not many sports can do that," says Martina.

"Many of my high-net-worth clients that I had at Fisher Island did business around pickleball."

Martina was amazed at how things happened.

"They would start their meeting on a court at nine o'clock in the morning with a one-hour lesson and some time for play."

She continues, "The rest of it was socializing and sort of an intro into their business before taking off for the country club or beach club where the real meeting took place."

"Pickleball is the new golf," says Martina.

"It's the new foursome where people would come in and you didn't really have to be at the same level in order to enjoy yourself, have fun. I saw a lot of that."

"The Special Forces group is just such a tight community," says Martina.

"When my husband would have an exercise and there would be Navy SEALs coming in, you could clearly see them having fun on the pickleball court."

She continues, "And I would try to connect military spouses to the game when the husbands were gone. It's a really nice kind of break from the kids and daily hustle."

For Martina, the game is now a passion.

"Like I said, anyone can play. Military life can be tough sometimes, and it's cheaper than therapy."

She continues, "And it's just really, really fun because endorphins give you happiness."

Martina knows the sport needs more women at the professional level.

"Anna Leigh is a different breed. She's like an overall athlete who has that rare combination of hard work and focus to go with the physical skills."

Martina continues, "She's such a prodigy, growing up in the sport instead of high-level tennis or other sports."

"I do think that the level of play has changed so much because of the equipment that is being manufactured," says Martina.

"Women can actually handle their part. Before, men would just take over points. Not now. Women are rising to the competition."

Pickleball is opening up new doors.

"I think it's a great opportunity to enter into pro sports," says Martina.

"If you're in a high school or collegiate team, just getting that experience counts. These young athletes have a big opportunity to evolve their game before making the next step."

She continues, "They can learn strategy and get comfortable before competing against the pros."

"Two of my clients at Fisher Island never played a sport in their lives," says Martina.

"Both started playing pickleball at 72, and came to the court saying, 'I don't like competition. I just want to come out there and play and have fun.' Last year one of them entered the U.S. Open."

Martina has also seen romance flourish on the court.

"I know people who met their spouses on pickleball courts. I know people who got engaged on a pickleball court. I know people who had a bridal shower on a pickleball court."

She continues, "It's not just a sport, it's a lifestyle. It brings people from all backgrounds together."

It really opens up a completely new world for someone who never has been exposed to sport even. But the most impressive is starting, both of the ladies started at 72, never played a sport in their life. I said, I'm sure you had. And you know what was funny? It was actually a little easier to teach than someone who had a golf or a tennis background.

Some people technically might not be as sound, but then when you get them on a court with no previous experience whatsoever, any kind of technical challenges, they literally do what you tell them, very simply explain how to mechanically hold a paddle, make a point of contact with the ball, where to stand. It's just life changing.

Martina has seen the amateur sport of pickleball shift to more of an emphasis on improving overall skills.

"Everyone is really concerned about their DUPR rating. Now we are seeing many more players focus on drilling and strategy. That's how the game has evolved."

"One day my extremely handsome 6'2", 215-pound husband who played rugby in college agreed to be the fourth in a lady's clinic. They were 70-plus and so sweet," says Martina.

"So, he jumped on the ferry to play, and when it was over he was drenched in sweat after losing to them. How's that for a humbling experience? He's a Green Beret and gets beat by some ladies who had never played any sport before."

We had members from Europe, from Asia. And these people had to learn how to communicate together. So that was really impressive seeing a hedge fund manager from New York City playing with a 72-year-old lady who helped him with court position and then going on to win a game together.

On a trip to Slovenia (where Martina is from), they visited the capital city.

"We taped some courts and had a great time. And I invited one of my college friends who was originally from Serbia but decided to make the move with the family from Houston to Ljubljana, to Slovenia."

Martina continues, "Afterwards, she asked how to bring pickleball to Slovenia. We helped her start some little camps and clinics, with Joola sponsoring it."

"The trip spurred all kinds of activity," said Martina.

"One of my friends decided to build four pickleball courts in a little mountain town as part of their rental property."

She continues, "Another boutique hotel is building multiple courts on its properties to attract travelers. It's such a small country, but they're really growing fast."

As the global ambassador for Dill Dinkers as well as Regional Developer for Tampa and Lakeland, Martina leads the charge for expansion.

"Our plans are to build 20-plus indoor facilities."

With a flexible model, they focus on creating between six to eighteen courts at each.

"We focus on quality nets, quality sound, good colors and lighting," says Martina.

"Core pickleball players want quality and we are committed to providing that."

She continues, "Players want to find games at a similar skill level, and that's hard to do at public courts."

Dill Dinkers also focuses on programming with leagues, clinics, corporate events, birthday parties, tournaments and lessons.

"I think these are all very important as a facility operator," says Martina.

"There are so many new people coming to the game, and we want to cater to all players."

"I love pickleball because it brings people together from all backgrounds and in the world. Anyone can play no matter the skill, age or race."

Matt Manasse

Pickleball Coach to the Stars

Before 2017, Matt had never even heard of pickleball. "When I first played in '20, I didn't understand the game at all."

It wasn't until the pandemic that the game made a return.

"My parents thought I had COVID and sent me back to Pennsylvania."

"After a month of being back in Pennsylvania alone, one of the people I used to play tennis with invited me to play pickleball."

Matt continues, "Someone opened up the local tennis center that had one court of pickleball and that's what people were starting to do."

This time around, the game clicked for him.

In Erie, lots of Matt's friends had never played a racket sport.

"I had tried to convince many of them to try pickleball. But it wasn't until my birthday that May that I convinced them to play."

He continues, "We did some dinking and some drinking. After that, everyone was addicted to the game."

"The two that were the most reluctant now run the Erie Pickleball Players Association," says Matt.

"They even own a club and most of their vacations revolve around either going to an MLP event or going to Mexico where there's pickleball courts. I think it's really brought them and the community closer together. So, to be a part of that transformation is really cool."

Matt started playing every day that summer.

"I was obsessed and quickly became one of the best players in my area."

He also started noticing his social media started blowing up with reels about pickleball.

"I was noticing some pro reels being posted. Then my buddy Tony Giannoni in Florida told me I should try and go pro."

"I got introduced to Ryan Sherry," says Matt.

"He was looking for a partner for an event in August in California. It was the first or second PPA event ever."

The next week Matt was in Florida training.

"We ended up partying more than practicing."

A clinic hosted by Ben Johns and Simone Jardim was happening, and Matt got an invitation to attend.

"Tony was hosting the clinic with Ben and Simone and housed all of us in Orlando for three days," says Matt.

"And I had only been playing pickleball for a few months."

Immersed with the best players in the world, Matt spent the entire weekend playing in the day and watching video at night.

"I was hooked."

"In August, I attended my first event in California and met Doug Ellin from *Entourage* at one of my first training sessions," says Matt.

"And that's when I was like, my God, pickleball is the networking sport, especially in California."

He continues, "I had the idea of starting the pickleball program at the Riviera Country Club. So, I moved out in October of 2020, a month or two after that first event here. And I was like; I'm going to use pickleball as a vehicle to figure my life out."

After his first week in California, Matt's vision was to use pickleball to get into the entertainment industry.

"That was the goal," says Matt.

"The Riviera Country Club had all the stars, all the producers and all the agents. I just didn't know it would come that quickly."

"My first real lesson there that actually got me the job was with four women," says Matt.

"I only knew their first names. After they left, I learned that three of them were Larry David's wife, Ari Emanuel's wife, and Jim Berkus' wife from UTA."

He continues, "They started taking lessons from me a couple times a week then they brought their husbands on the weekend and that turned into my original Sunday crew."

"I think my time in California and the constant hustle changed my life, while being exposed to new situations and people," says Matt.

"It's given me some notoriety, allowed me to learn a lot of stuff on the business side and gave me a voice on the commentary side of things that I never had," says Matt.

"But I think it's helped a lot of people in a lot of good ways. I'm a part of a couple different charities that have changed from tennis events to now pickleball events."

Matt has an iconic picture at the country club.

"It was like Larry sitting next to Jim Berkus sitting next to Ari Emanuel."

He continues, "UTA and WME are rival agencies and using my favorite *Entourage* as my guide, Ari Gold wouldn't be caught dead sitting next to the head of another agency in real life. This happened because of pickleball."

"Wilson was my sponsor at the time and made me twenty-five custom paddles that I could hand out as gifts," says Matt.

"That was my first foray into the celebrity scene. After that, I became known as the coach to the stars."

With Matthew Perry as one of his first big clients, Matt soon had his own article in *Vanity Fair*.

"It was a great piece, and all about me. You just kind of ride the wave from there," he said.

"Soon I got approached by a friend who was trying to get the Tennis Channel to start airing pickleball."

"A couple of months later, I did a clinic for Bob Wiley, Ken Solomon and the whole C-suite of the Tennis Channel," said Matt.

"Not soon after that, pickleball was on the network."

In need of commentators, Matt joined the team.

"It's been a couple of years now. I really enjoy being the on-camera face for Pickleball TV."

"So, in golf in the 80s, people would say, 'If you want to know what someone's really about, take them out on a golf course and play a game. It's going to show their true colors'," says Matt.

"I don't know if that's also true on a pickleball court, but I have definitely seen some people react differently when playing."

But for Matt, the pickleball court is always a place of comfort.

"You can be yourself. Even if you have a bad day and act in an obnoxious manner. Normally, right afterwards, everyone forgives each other, and you move on."

"It's funny. Pickleball is a frustrating game, because I never know what I love most about it," says Matt.

"It's a great workout, and the social scene for pickleball in LA is great."

He continues, "And then the mental game is just as interesting with the strategy, learning how to play with a new partner, and even how you have to constantly change your tactic. There's something very addicting about the game."

Matt knows the industry is still early.

"The recreational side continues to grow. There are 65,000 courts in the U.S. right now."

He continues, "The age demographic continues to get younger and younger, which is good. And I do think more people are watching the sport than ever before."

"It's still one of those things where people enjoy playing pickleball a lot more than watching others," says Matt.

"It will take time to build the viewers and appreciation of the sport. I think that the college programs will help fans connect better with the next generation of pro players."

The market is finally stepping up to meet the demand.

"Pickleball TV is doing a lot to try to create some more original content," says Matt.

"They actually created a dating show that's going to be announced soon."

"Andy Roddick, Ben Stiller and Jake Johnson will be in a movie called *The Dink*," says Matt.

"One of my buddies was a body double in it. And I'm in *Pickleheads*, which is a mockumentary drama where I play myself as a commentator with John O'Hurley."

Matt was also involved in a CBS special with Stephen Colbert which aired in '22.

"I don't know how many people even watched it, but I felt the show did a huge disservice to pickleball," says Matt.

"My hope is there's more and more of these documentaries and people see what the sport is, how community driven it is and how athletic it can be. And hopefully it just keeps growing."

Known as the "Pickleball Coach to the Stars," Matt has lots of great memories.

"I traveled with Emma Watson for three weeks in Europe. That was amazing."

He continues, "And the first time I ever hung out with Jamie Foxx, we shut down Maestro's Steakhouse after our two-hour pickleball game at Westlake Tennis Club. I'm so fortunate to have experienced moments like these."

With the game slowly gaining popularity, many have felt celebrities aren't needed to grow the sport.

"The bottom line is that our culture really loves celebrities," says Matt.

"Jamie Foxx has talked about that all the time. Hollywood will always be here. And if they care about pickleball, it can help our sport grow."

"We are always interviewing celebrities on Pickleball TV," says Matt.

"I've done episodes with people like Drew Brees and Katie Couric. Hopefully, that will shine some light on the game."

Matt hopes to soon do an event with the Matthew Perry Foundation.

"Pickleball is something that's a really nice escape for him. It's definitely something that I'm proud of as the sport is pretty therapeutic and fun."

So, what about his nickname McNasty?

"In high school, one of my coaches at Evert Tennis Academy in Florida, Christian Kawas, would have me run the lake whenever I acted out or talked back," says Matt.

"And he would be like, all right, go run McNasty. I don't know why McNasty became my name then, but it kind of stuck through high school into college."

"When I got into pickleball, the first event I ever played on the PPA tour was in California," says Matt.

"People in the draw had nicknames like the Flying Frenchman, the Flying Unicorn, and Johnny Pickleball."

So, Matt chose the name Pickleball McNasty. And it stuck.

After appearing in a few articles, Matt decided to lean into it.

"I think it's a fun brand. I actually have the copyrights to all of it, including eight different logos and we're going to do some fun stuff with K-Swiss later this year and we'll see where it goes."

Mattias Johannson
The Pickleball OG

"Before COVID, I was completely focused on being the number one player in the world in the forty-five-year age group. I had one more tournament left (the World Championship in Miami) and only needed to reach the quarterfinal to solidify my ranking," says Mattias.

"And then, the pandemic hit."

"The only thing that was open was pickleball, and I got asked by a friend to play."

"They explained the game to me. I had no interest, but my friend wouldn't stop asking," says Mattias.

"So, after the third time I said yes. I mean, how many hours can you spend cleaning the house and the garage?"

"As soon as we started playing, the fascination of the game hit me."

"I was just intrigued by how a couple of ladies could play that well, as I was a very accomplished tennis player. The finesse and everything else really intrigued me."

"So, we had to play pickleball."

"She was also a longtime tennis player and laughed at the suggestion."

"Now my wife is a pickleball addict too."

"My wife and I started playing socially at Worthy Park in Huntington Beach, and at a friend's condo where they taped the tennis courts up to play pickleball," says Mattias.

"After a few months, the game was getting too easy, and I needed some stronger competition."

"I went to Las Vegas, one of the biggest PPA tournaments not really knowing what was going on."

"After winning a few rounds, I played Scott Moore and lost to him in three games. It really upset me."

"And then, my name gets called again," says Mattias.

"I had been put in a back draw, not even knowing what it meant."

"It was after the fact that I found out you could play your way back into the draw. I chalked it up as a learning experience for the next tournament."

"Basically, 99% of my friends are from the game. And we do lots more than just play the game. Our whole social circle has changed."

"It's so easy to find the right people to hang out with while playing this game."

"I'm decent enough that the young pros still want to practice with me," says Mattias.

"I have the luxury of both worlds where I can play with them during the week, and my wife and friends on the weekend."

"I had my knee replacement done in December, and I didn't expect it to be that hard to come back to the top level," says Mattias.

"Sometimes I wonder how long I'll do this. It's a lot of traveling. But when you are passionate about something, you want to keep doing it."

"If I can hold on to that number one spot one more year and then potentially shift a bit more to doubles. I still want to play and win, no matter what. But now, the Master division (60+) is looking a bit more appealing."

"Maybe I will start over again and compete at the Masters Pro Division," says Mattias.

"I don't think I'm going anywhere soon, as far as not competing and wanting to do this. This is the drive of my life. You know, it's too much fun to give up."

"When you are ranked number one, you get a lot of requests for lessons and clinics and traveling to different countries and in different areas. So, I do teach quite a lot of pickleball," says Mattias.

"I get called a lot from tennis players who want to play the game. Often, they understand the basics and the strategy and just need help with technique," says Mattias.

"Things continue to evolve in pickleball, but most who I teach can very quickly go out and play at the 4.5 level."

"When I played pickleball with my college kids on the last day of the season, none of them had really played pickleball before and they were not very good in the first 10–15 minutes."

"But at the end of two hours, they picked it up so well that I told two of them that with some practice they could play at the pro level."

"I've seen a lot of people who maybe were overweight, not in shape, maybe socially distanced or not very sociable at that time. And they really come to life playing pickleball."

"I probably know of at least four or five guys who were very overweight when they started and now, they shed 50–100 pounds. You can see the transformation and the self-confidence come back. It's awesome."

"I don't think there is another sport where you can come alone to a pickleball club for the first time, play with strangers, and leave with a few phone numbers of those wanting to play again," says Mattias.

"Pickleball is a fun, relaxing and welcoming community. There's no other sport like it with this kind of social interaction."

"I see people there at the club that live there," says Mattias.

"They are there two times a day and they play three, four hours each day. I mean, it's almost like an addiction to the sport."

"Now everybody gets irritated if you have to check your phone, and you have to apologize. The phone is gone when you play pickleball, which is fantastic."

"They were really there to gamble but also signed up for our clinic (me and Vince Van Patten)."

"I saw the passion and the drive with them, and we are still in contact today, we really had nothing in common. But pickleball brought us together. It's pretty amazing."

"When you go to tournaments now, it's too much towards just what the pros are doing," says Mattias.

"If you really look at it, the amateurs are paying for the pros. But they get the worst courts, the worst playing times, and always have their matches cancelled first with weather issues."

"At the tournaments, I've heard many players say that they would not come back and play again," says Mattias.

"The game needs to be more inclusive and listen to what's being said. Otherwise, you will see the numbers at future tournaments drop."

"The generation coming in now started playing when they were 8-10 years old," says Mattias.

"They have only known pickleball and will be unbelievably good. This will change the game. They are going to see different nuances of the game that we never have."

"It was more like a big party the whole time," he says.

"When you were done, people went to the bar and ate and drank and they stayed around and watched the other games and just enjoyed it."

"Now it's less engaging than what it was before. And I think the engagement factor is necessary."

"Obviously, the game is now driven by money, and that's why they do it," says Mattias.

"But the amateurs or wheelchair players deserve a few minutes of fame, too. If the matches were on center court and a wheelchair came in, I would have stayed and watched it because I'm interested in how good these people are with the two bounces and how they maneuver that wheelchair back and forward."

"Now they are out on the outer courts most of the time, and nobody sees the games because they don't get any TV time."

"It's too bad that the different tours took the senior pros off of TV," says Mattias.

"We used to be on the center court, we used to be streamed, we used to be on TV. But the APP and PPA decided no one wants to watch us."

"I can't tell you how often I meet people who ask where they can watch me and other senior pros play."

"It's my opinion that older players want to see us play and compare what is possible in our age to do. Most don't care about how good Ben Johns is, because we can never accomplish that. It might be great to watch once in a while, but most want to see what is possible with their game."

"With icons like Andre Agassi now driving the sport, the 40 to 60-year-old fans are paying the money for the young pros to play, and they probably should realize that but so far they haven't," says Mattias.

"One time, I got invited to play pickleball with Andre Agassi," says Mattias.

"So when I told Andre that I was coming to Las Vegas, and I would grab a rental car and be at his place by 1 p.m.. He offered to pick me up at the airport."

"I politely declined, but it shows what a genuine person he is."

"He didn't get mad about it, cause he's such a humble and nice guy overall. The owner shifted a lesson, and we were able to play," says Mattias.

"But the moral of this story is: no matter who you are, be nice. It always makes a difference. I'll always remember how this iconic legend and his wife (Steffi) are so laid back, so considerate, and so genuine."

"I love pickleball because it has transformed people's lives, from a mental, physical and social aspect. And it's such a genius game that is so easy to learn, but so difficult to master."

Megan Fudge

A Family Affair

"Tennis was my first love, the reason I came to America, and how I met my husband Ryler," says Megan.

"During COVID we relocated to St Pete from Orlando when Ryler was let go as the national coach for Team USA."

"I had enough of tennis, and was working in the insurance world."

"We started getting invitations to go play pickleball, meet other couples and get some exercise," says Megan.

"It was challenging but also fascinating, and we both thought we could be good at it. And so our pickleball career started."

"Coming back to our home every week was draining with the dogs, the kids, the cleaning, the laundry, packing and doing it over and over again."

"We didn't feel like it was sustainable as a family for us to do it week in and week out with the two kids," says Megan.

"JR was four at the time and Lily was six, and we were trying to figure out how to take our home with us where we don't feel like we are always living out of a suitcase and just surviving."

"They weren't doing it full time but were having great adventures. So, I asked Ryler what he thought about a home on wheels."

"He vetoed me instantly, and said we're not handy people, have an RV, and wouldn't know what we were doing."

"As the airline and hotel bills kept adding up, the idea started to slowly grow. Ryler agreed we should go look at an RV."

"We haven't looked back since," says Megan.

"We've been in the RV full time for two years now and revamped our lives to the point where we've become minimalists."

"It was liberating to get rid of stuff we didn't need and just focus on what was important."

"It has been important to us to be on this journey together," says Megan.

"Meeting more people and growing the sport and going after this passion that we found in this incredible sport has given us another life."

"It's just become something fun and is continually evolving. Right now, we are working on a pickleball blog."

"I was just telling Ryler how I would love to be on a hike right now rather than playing pickleball. We love to be in nature, so the RV life kinda works for us," says Megan.

"Back when I was in insurance and Ryler was coaching, we would escape to pickleball."

"Now I see all these trails in the middle of Tennessee and can't wait to go on them. That's our getaway, our outlet, our exercise."

"My wheels are constantly turning on what's the next step, the next move, the next country we can travel to, the next thing that we can support, help grow, put our passion behind, and positively impact this world a little bit."

"We have lots of projects in the works. Always."

"I'm working on branding, branching out into running tournaments and events, our kids' journeys, and how else we can help the international platform for Franklin," says Megan.

"It's a lot, but that's how I like it. Thankfully Ryler likes to keep things simple, and talks about what's for dinner, and where we are driving to."

"They looked a little rough around the edges and Ryler smiled at me," says Megan.

"He couldn't get through all the motorcycles in front of us and wanted me to go out and ask if they would move. I was like, are you serious?!"

"So, I jumped out of our RV, completely forgetting it was wrapped in the Franklin logo, and asked them to move."

"They asked if I played pickleball, and I started smiling."

"Turns out most of them are also pickleball players. I'm no longer intimidated, and we start talking about the game."

"Normally, we're off site nowadays. It's been kind of nice to get a little bit more peace and quiet," says Megan.

"We definitely check in and have a lot of friends on the staff side of the APP tour. The kids love to help with the volunteer booths. The APP has done a phenomenal job of making my kids feel part of their family."

"It's nice that a lot of people recognize them now," says Megan.

"Whether we're traveling around the country or the world, people are like, 'You're Megan's kids or Ryler's kids.' Sometimes that comes with a burden, but they've been handling it really well."

"The kids (8 and 10) amaze me. I don't take for granted that we're on this journey thanks to them," says Megan.

"They've been very open minded about traveling to different countries and meeting different people. They enjoy the sport, and they love competing."

"Sometimes Lily has had enough and needs a break, or JR wants to do something else."

"But for right now, we're just hoping to use this pickleball vessel to show them the world, and that if you go after your passion and your dreams, that something amazing can happen."

"People share this bizarre interaction when it comes to pickleball. It creates this common ground," says Megan.

"Even when we were in India the kids were able to make friends on the court. They didn't speak the same language but understood an invitation to play."

"In what other situation could we be in, where we would go to another country, and our kids can make friends with people that they can't talk to? But they have this common ground with pickleball. It's just so fun. It's so fascinating."

"JR was determined to get into open play because he hadn't played in a while," says Megan.

"There's all these like 40, 50, 60 old men and women playing."

"When we come back a few hours later he's sitting at the bar with a man in his 60s and they are sharing life stories."

"I asked JR what he was doing, and he said it was his buddy from pickleball," says Megan.

"He told me they were talking and playing and decided to get something to drink after. The two were talking about traveling. How awesome is that?"

"We're definitely very passionate about the youth side," says Megan.

"It hits home for us, creating a pathway for our kids, but also for juniors and kids to come. We've always been in high-performance junior coaching. Ryler was a national coach for Team USA in the junior section. I ran our high-performance program on the junior side."

"So I just know that if we can grow the market on the youth side, it will elevate the game level drastically if we can get players coming out earlier."

"Their athleticism is off the charts. Boys are playing pickleball who would normally be playing football, basketball and baseball, which are traditional American sports."

"Now they're choosing pickleball. It's cool. That's really exciting to me."

"Last year when I was in India, I spoke to a group of girls that were training and competing at this academy," says Megan.

"And I was like, girls, this is our sport. This is our platform. This is our way of equal pay, equal opportunity, equal power in the game. We are one of the most viewed competitions as women's doubles. We are excited to watch this sport, and you can really go after it."

"It's more than any other sport in the world right now. We're making an impact and we're making enough money to be able to do this."

"I would love to get out there. My dad's originally from New Zealand, so I have family there," says Megan.

"They want to see me compete in Australia and New Zealand. They've been following my journey very closely the last couple of months, but the schedules for 2025 have not aligned, unfortunately, thus far."

"He was a squash player growing up, gained 100 pounds, and went into deep depression going through divorce," says Megan.

"This man was ready to take his life when he got invited to play pickleball."

"Nobody talks about pickleball in Germany or very, very little," says Megan.

"So, this man decided he had nothing to lose and showed up for a game. As soon as he met people, he exercised and found a passion in something again. It sparked something in him."

"And he's on this life revamp now. We met him 12 months in and he's like 50 pounds lighter and he has this group of people around him that he meets every Tuesday and Thursday. He has a new inspiration in life."

"Pickleball was so impactful for people post-COVID, because it gave them an outlet, an inspiration, a social network, and a reason to go outside," says Megan.

"It gave people hope again. The sport has changed the world. It's only continuing to do that. I think it's one of the most inclusive sports there is."

"I love pickleball because it's brought us as a family closer together. There is not another profession where I would be able to do this with my family, with my kids, with my husband on the road, competing in the same sport as them, coaching the sport, growing the game together, being ambassadors together. There's nothing, there's no way."

Mehvish Safdar

The Doctor of Pickleball

Entering a grueling stretch of her sport psychology PhD program, Mehvish was also dealing with the start of COVID.

"I was really sedentary and was just going through a particularly difficult season of life."

A lifelong tennis player, she knew that it was time for a new activity. Living in Bloomington, Indiana, Mehvish went on Google in search of pickleball.

"I found Timber Tucker's name, and he immediately got me involved with a group that played. He has been a big part of my pickleball journey."

"Everything took off from there as I started playing for the Indiana University Pickleball Club team in the fall of 2023. Timber has put so much energy into developing the competitive aspect of the IU club team and growing the collegiate pickleball scene in general," says Mehvish.

"It's amazing what he's done in such a short amount of time for IU and beyond."

In the final phase of her PhD program, Mehvish has her dissertation and clinical internship left before receiving this designation.

"It's a long journey that I signed up for," says Mehvish.

"It's fortunate that these two paths ended up kind of coming together for me."

For Mehvish, it's a delicate balance.

"Not many people on tour are advancing two careers at the same time. I think five years from now I would ideally want to still be doing a mix of sport psychology work and pickleball."

She continues, "The cool thing is that my sport psychology career and pro pickleball career are quite compatible and I hope to merge the two. I'd probably work with an organization or do private practice."

"I think the reason I ended up signing with the tour was I wanted to know if I had what it took to be amongst the best in the world," says Mehvish.

"I didn't want any regrets looking back, wondering if I had what it took. So, I'll keep training, keep improving, and keep competing to see how far I can go."

During Mehvish's time as a pro, she has enjoyed having people reach out and wish her good luck.

"It's been really cool. Even if I don't advertise that I'm playing a tournament or my results, people follow along on their own and share words of encouragement."

"I like that the PPA hosts the pro division and amateur division at the same venue during the same time," she says.

"The amateur players get to interact with pro players, helping them realize we are normal people, fostering connection and relatability amongst the pickleball community."

So far, Mehvish has only played pickleball in the U.S.

"I'll do an international tour stop within the next year, but I haven't figured out which one yet. The PPA tour has recently expanded greatly internationally and pickleball continues to expand worldwide."

"When we're on court, it's all business," says Mehvish.

"You might be best friends with the person you're across the court from, but you're trying to win that match and doing whatever it takes. We're all competitive out there. But in between, people are really nice and friendly."

"The tournament schedule is pretty packed with matches and doing things to prepare for them. It's hard to find much outside time to do other things."

"But people do enjoy doing simple things like eating meals or just playing a card game at the hotel or Airbnb with fellow players."

She continues, "A lot of times players will also stay together. So that off-court time often fosters further camaraderie."

"It's cool and unique that we get to play alongside and compete against the opposing gender," says Mehvish.

"It's not too often that you're playing a professional sport and the other gender is involved in one of the events."

"Yeah, I think that us touring pros do have to be pretty flexible and go with the flow. And I think most players are pretty understanding that this is new territory and adjustments are going to have to be made as the tour learns," says Mehvish.

"But the PPA Tour does a good job of communicating changes."

"I have what I consider a pretty moderate training schedule in comparison to other tour players," says Mehvish.

"But for me personally, I find it important to have a life balance. So right now, I play five days a week for two hours a day. The balance allows me to enjoy pickleball more and perform better."

For now, Mehvish is sticking to her schedule.

"It might change as I figure out what's best for me, but I like to stick to my time boundaries."

"I don't know the exact stats, but I've definitely seen the average age of pickleball players getting younger and younger," says Mehvish.

"The tour still has a wide age range, which is really cool, but I do think it's gaining the attention of younger athletes more and more."

Now full time in pickleball, Mehvish is excited to see the growth.

"The sport is just booming. Driving around North Carolina, where I live right now, the local parks are always packed."

She continues, "There are people waiting in line at the courts to get on. So many are continuing to fall in love with pickleball which was historically seen as an old people sport."

"Pickleball is something that is very accessible to a lot of people," says Mehvish.

"You can get started pretty easily and learn the basics by getting your hands on a paddle and stepping out on a court."

Mehvish knows the impact it can have on disadvantaged populations.

"We just did a youth clinic in Atlanta at a recent tour stop with an underserved population of youth that had never touched a paddle before," says Mehvish.

"The joy on their faces getting to hit this plastic ball around and doing it with their friends and just being outside was a really meaningful experience. And I think that speaks to the positive impact that it can make on the world."

Mehvish's whole family has played pickleball.

"My older, middle sister has been playing at the pro level as well and we've been doubles partners."

She continues, "My family in general is very athletic, so they were able to pick up pickleball pretty quickly. Sometimes when I'm home we will go to a Lifetime and play. It's been fun to connect over pickleball as a family."

"Something that I feel pretty passionate about is mental health and mindset in general," says Mehvish.

"Mental health is something that's often overlooked and being active is something we know helps people with their mental health. Pickleball is something that can help people who are struggling with different mental health issues."

"I love pickleball because it's really just allowed me to compete and also connect. It's provided me with new friendships, new opportunities, new challenges, and new ways to positively impact the world."

Michael "Sleeves" Sliwa

Pickleball Maniac

"I was on vacation in Lake Tahoe with my extended family during the first summer of COVID," Michael said.

"An athletic family, we would always go hiking. But this time, my niece's boyfriend brought a bunch of paddles and wanted to introduce us to the game of pickleball."

"They had four courts, so we hit it around for about an hour and a half," Michael said.

"When am I ever going to play this again? I live in the middle of nowhere in a yurt with some really old tennis courts out there."

"About a year later, I came to find out that somebody had painted pickleball lines on our crumbling 50-year-old tennis courts," Michael said.

"So, I just showed up for about a week waiting for the people who painted the lines to show up and they finally did. It was a British couple that had been playing for a few years."

Now Michael is part of a group of about 25 players.

"Twice a week, the group plays on some 'rough' courts. They are really bad. We just have temporary nets and call it the world's worst pickleball courts," says Michael.

"The court is barely holding on, and parts of it fall off all the time. So, we have to piece it back together because you can't replace the court."

He continues, "We love the game so much, our rag tag group will play in the worst possible conditions."

"I'm right up against the Gila Wilderness in New Mexico. There's not a lot of stuff out here," says Michael.

"Our closest actual courts are in Silver City, which is 35 miles away. Sometimes we treat ourselves to games there, even though we still have to use temporary nets."

"Right now, they're working on getting some permanent pickleball courts at the university. They are building a recreation center with a gym floor too, so we can play when it's oppressively hot outside," Michael said.

"Every few weeks, I play at my friend's private court."

"I'm a huge fan of watching the pro game at any level," Michael said.

"My YouTube channel covers the senior pro game, and I watch a lot of their tournaments and league matches. I'm all about watching good players, whether on the APP, MLP or PPA tours."

"Along with that, the channel takes up a lot of my time reviewing paddles and interviewing personalities around the game. There's always plenty to do."

He continues, "I think it's pretty fascinating all the walks of life that kind of come to this. That has really kept me interested because it's always changing with the game, the players, and the technology."

"I've been interviewing consistently for about three years now," Michael said.

"I haven't counted, but if I had to guess, I'd say about 120 guests total. Some of my most recent include NBA Hall of Famer Rick Barry and Joe Gannascoli, who played Vito on the Sopranos. Both of them had so much energy and enthusiasm for the game. It was cool."

"This market is blowing up because seniors can play pickleball at all levels," Michael said.

"It gives them the most choices to play, whether in the APP, PPA or on their own in leagues like the National Pickleball League. People are always surprised when I tell them this."

"Pickleball is super welcoming," Michael said.

"I've never been involved in a sport where when you walk up to a court, even if you don't even have a paddle, somebody will get you one and sometimes give you one for good. And it's not that hard to learn."

He remembers a woman who showed up with a ball and paddle.

"She would hit against the wall just because it was good exercise and she had no desire to really come and play and compete. She did that for months and months and months."

"Even if you've never played a ball sport and are terrified of sports in general because of your memories of P.E. in high school, you can play pickleball," Michael said.

"When they hit a ball with this paddle, something lights up with them. It went over the net, it stayed in, and it didn't bounce over the fence. So, they didn't look like fools."

"It's sort of this commonality you play pickle and I think that's super cool. I played beach volleyball for 25 years and that is not a welcoming environment. That is super cliquey. It takes you years to kind of break into the good group and to get in."

"I'm not saying pickleball doesn't have some of those things, but at the end of the day, I think a lot of folks realize what we're doing. We're just playing a goofy wiffle ball game and having a good time. And it's kind of an escape from what's going on around us in the world domestically and abroad. So, it's a good place to kind of just be in a bubble."

"I enjoy living the simple life in a yurt," Michael said.

"What I own, I could pack up in my car. It doesn't take a ton of money to live out here in the middle of nowhere."

He continues, "I don't really have a plan for my pickleball future. Opportunities come my way all the time, the last one being the movie 'Dreambreaker: A Pickleball Story'."

"I was asked by the filmmakers to go to the Major League Pickleball event in Mesa, Arizona in early 2023 to see if I could briefly speak with MLP founder Steve Kuhn," Michael said.

"The place was packed, and Steve was busy chatting so I formed a plan. I was going to wait until he went to the restroom and then at the sink just congratulate him on the success of the league and event."

He continues, "I would later approach him hoping he would recognize me from earlier and grant me an opportunity to briefly interview him."

"Hours later when the finals were about to start in the stadium court, he walked out to stretch his legs, so I quickly approached him and introduced myself."

"He was kind enough to give me a few minutes. After a few questions I got to the main one which was really just something to get a reaction."

"Having explained to him that I lived off grid in a yurt (a really nice tent) and below the poverty level (voluntarily) for many years, I then asked if he knew what a yurt was?" Michael said.

"He replied he did and so I asked him what the financing would look like for someone like me to purchase a MLP franchise? He laughed out loud and then replied, 'A whole bunch of yurts!' I thanked him for his time, and he shook my hand and walked away."

Michael's social media footprint continues to grow from the movie exposure and his podcast, The Senior Pickleball Report.

"I make some money off of paddle reviews and just got involved in a pickleball travel business. No matter what the outcome, I'm still happy hitting this ball and having a good time."

"Looking back on the club system in golf, there was the men's night, there was the women's night, there was the mixed night."

"I think not just for safety, but for other reasons, you're going to see a little bit more segmentation in some pickleball circles."

"There is definitely a movement in the game where different age groups organize games their own way," Michael said.

"The younger crowd uses things like Playtime Scheduler, and the older group just shows up for open play. With the level of play increasing, skill groups are starting to separate, and that's OK."

"I just like to play and sometimes work on a skill. It's nice not to worry about winning."

He continues, "Part of pickleball is helping others with their game and even showing newbies how to play. That's really fun too!"

"When people find out I have a podcast, I give them paddles to try and even keep," Michael said.

"There's this very giving feeling I get when I come on to a court that I've never experienced anywhere else."

"I think they're doing a decent job with changing camera angles so you can see the speed of the ball, especially during dinks and cross-court shots."

"You need to bring the viewer down to the court a little more instead of just the old behind-the-baseline shot of the whole court."

"At some point, the players have to stop calling their own lines. I mean, this is absurd," Michael said.

"And I would love to have more players and coaches mic'd up. It would be fun to hear what they are saying to each other. Pickleball should be its own kind of sport."

"There is more interaction between the players, which I think is really cool. And people who start playing get better over time. They can see the nuances of the game, and some shots they couldn't do before."

"But players also realize the skill of the pros and know they could never be that good."

"I'd like to see more neighborhoods host block parties like we used to have," Michael said.

"It would be a great way to bring the game to the kids, the neighbors, and the community and have tons of fun doing it."

He continues, "Just lay down some lines, set up a net, and get started. Can you imagine raising money for a good cause, doing a little exhibition, then handing out paddles for anyone to try pickleball?"

"I love pickleball simply because it's the only game I've ever played where the fellow players are as enjoyable as the game itself."

Mick Tingstrom

A Game of Giving

A trip home for Christmas to Colorado Springs in 2019 brought Mick an unexpected gift.

"My dad said he wanted to introduce me to a new sport called 'Pickleball.' I had never heard of it, and my initial response was ... that sounds lame!"

"The next thing I know, my dad hands me and my kids a paddle and within ten minutes, my dad (77), me (51), my daughter (23), and my son (11) — essentially four generations — were going at it like it was Game 7 of the World Series!"

Mick was immediately hooked! When he returned to Washington, DC, he wasted no time signing up for a local pickleball tournament that was happening in a few months.

"When I went online to register, it told me I had to be a member of USA Pickleball, and without consulting my wife, instead of paying the $25 annual membership fee to play in the tournament, believing I would play pickleball until the day I die, I decided it would be a better 'deal' to spend $500 for the lifetime membership."

"In the morning, my wife saw a $500+ charge on our credit card and thought I was absolutely nuts for spending that much money just to enter a pickleball tournament — especially given I had NO experience in the game."

"After explaining myself, and because she knew my lifelong passion for sport and competition, she quickly became the best supporter anyone could ask for. So that's how it all started."

Mick was part of a new cohort of pickleball players who started playing during the early days of COVID.

"A lot of folks were looking to do some activity outdoors, and pickleball offered the perfect way to get in a workout while social distancing and having fun," says Mick.

"But what I didn't know was how addictive the sport can be. There was one time early on when my wife said, 'You know, you've been playing pickleball for 10 days in a row.' And I'm like, no, I didn't, but if you are saying that you would like me to stay home tonight, I am happy to do that? But if not..., can I go play pickleball tonight?"

"That's sort of been my journey since the beginning."

Mick credits his parents and three brothers for helping him fall in love with sports at a young age and learn important life skills such as the importance of discipline, giving one's best, and being a good teammate.

"Not only did I compete with and alongside my brothers in pretty much everything from football, basketball, baseball, soccer, and swimming, but even the small things like who could eat the most number of pancakes or bowls of cereal in any given morning. Who would have thought that that was a gift?"

Because Mick grew up playing so many different sports, when he later had his own children, he was able to pass on the gift of sport to Tyler, Britney, and Matthew. For nearly two decades, Mick coached his three children in various youth sports and then later pickleball, passing on the gift of sports like his own father did for him.

In addition to having a love for sports, Mick has a deep love for Veterans. Following a successful 27-year career in the United States Army, Mick says:

"God gave me a gift I never expected … the opportunity to not only compete in pickleball, spend time with family playing pickleball, but also teach pickleball to Veterans."

After moving his family from Washington, DC to Colorado Springs to be closer to his parents, Mick shared that in the spring of 2023, he went to a one-day Veteran badminton and pickleball clinic in the local area hosted by the Military Adaptive Court Sports (MACS), which is a 501(c)(3) that provides racket sports rehabilitation programming for Veterans.

"The guy running the clinic was the top badminton player in the U.S. at one time and actually ran the USA Olympics badminton in Atlanta back in 1996, but he didn't know pickleball nearly as much as I did, so I offered to teach the session."

"There were several Veterans playing in a wheelchair, and when I saw how much joy it brought them, I left that session incredibly inspired, motivated, and with a commitment to give the gift of pickleball to my fellow Veterans," says Mick.

"Almost immediately after the clinic ended, I reached out to MACS and offered to be their permanent pickleball instructor in the Colorado Springs area. I then partnered with Lifetime (Fitness) and later Peak Pickleball (a world-class 24-indoor court facility) to obtain weekly access to indoor pickleball courts. In just 2.5

years, between my dad and I, we've taught and or facilitated regular weekly instruction and play for over 250 Veterans."

"One time, I had just finished up a Veteran pickleball clinic and there were two athletic teenagers who were just starting to play singles pickleball on an adjacent court. They were actually quite good."

"I asked them if my wheelchair partner and I could play a game against them, and they tried brushing us off. I told them to give us a chance, and they chuckled and reluctantly agreed."

"He has played in the U.S. Open every year, and he loves pickleball so much that he regularly drives down from Denver to Colorado Springs one to two times a week to play," said Mick.

"We absolutely whooped their butts! The kids couldn't believe it."

"I told them to make sure to go home tonight and tell your mom and dad that you got whooped by a guy in a wheelchair and an old guy in his late fifties."

"It was good-hearted, but great to show the kids how the older generation and people with physical limitations can come together to compete and play this great game."

To Mick, giving pickleball instruction to Veterans has and continues to be a gift and a highlight of his week.

"The smiles, the laughter, seeing relationships formed on and off the court is heartwarming and life-giving."

"Pickleball is a catalyst. And thanks to the generosity of individuals and non-profit and for-profit organizations like MACS, Lifetime, Peak Pickleball, Mt. Carmel Veterans Center, and so many more, Veterans are coming together for fun, fitness, and fellowship every week."

Staring at the contact list on his phone, Mick chuckles.

"I can guarantee you I have at least 600 to 700 people on my contact list with the last name 'Pickleball.' My kids tease me and say that I go to the 'Church of Pickleball' because I'm a pickleball preacher, a teacher, and a community advocate and activist."

"I'm the crazy guy who spent countless hours leading a successful multi-year campaign to convince the City of Colorado Springs to put 18 to 20 pickleball courts in the master plan for the next public park."

Mick is a driving force in growing the sport of wheelchair pickleball in Colorado and beyond. In 2023, he partnered with the Pikes Peak Pickleball Association (PPPA) to organize and run the first ever wheelchair pickleball tournament played in a major regional tournament in the State of Colorado.

"In just two years, we doubled the participation in the wheelchair divisions (which included singles, doubles, and hybrid — which is one player in a chair and one able-bodied player) with players coming from all over Colorado and as far as Hawaii, California, Utah, Wyoming, Arizona, New Mexico, and Minnesota."

Following the highly successful 2025 Colorado Open Pikes Peak or Bust Tournament, Mick knows that they are making wheelchair pickleball history.

"If you believe in miracles, several of us can envision a Wheelchair Pickleball National or World Championship someday being offered — maybe even right here in Colorado Springs."

While Mick spends much of his time giving pickleball instruction, he also competes in local through national-level sport competitions.

"Since turning 50, I have been joining my dad, Ray, in competing in the National Senior Games (NSG) multi-sport competitions —

to include the Huntsman World Games and my favorite event, the annual National Veteran Golden Age Games (NVGAG), which is held each year in a major U.S. city for Veterans over the age of 55."

"While my dad and I have earned nearly 200 medals in 10 different sports including pickleball, swimming, shuffleboard, badminton, cycling, powerwalk, table tennis, cornhole, and basketball free-throw shooting, more important and rewarding is our time together as father and son, and the special relationships we've formed with athletes and Veterans all over the country."

So, what's next? Mick has lofty plans.

"If all goes well, in the next 12 months, in addition to doing my full-time job and spending time with family, a year from now, I will see my youngest son, Matthew, enjoying his freshman year of college;" he said.

"I will have won a pickleball national championship at the 2025 USA Pickleball Nationals in San Diego; helped my swim team, Club Tribe, win a national championship at the 2026 U.S. Masters Swimming Spring National Championships in Greensboro, NC; medaled in the 2026 National Veterans Golden Age Games in Tampa, FL; taught or facilitated pickleball play for hundreds of Veterans, and helped organize and run a national-level wheelchair exclusive pickleball tournament. Besides that, nothing planned in 2026!" Mick said.

For Mick, pickleball and sport in general has and continues to be life-giving.

"While individual accomplishments are nice, medals fade and just sit in the closet or on a wall. What matters most is the positive impact you can have on someone else's life — both on and off the court. So, as you are able, get out there and give the gift of your time, talent, or treasure — you won't regret it."

Noah Suemnick

Faith in Pickleball

"Pickleball kind of fell into my lap around COVID. It's the same story with a lot of people," says Noah.

"In 2020, we were sent back home from college, and I had nothing to do. One of my buddies mentioned pickleball, which I thought was a stupid name. But then we went out to play and I was immediately addicted!"

"I wanted to bring pickleball back to my school," he says.

"The first year was pretty slow."

"When everyone went home for break, the kids started playing with their parents and friends. Everyone started talking about it," says Noah.

"In our second year, we grew to almost 200 players and became the biggest club on campus. This helped spark the idea of the National Collegiate Pickleball Association. I thought, why not make it bigger?"

"With no pickleball courts, setting up for games was a nightmare," says Noah.

"We needed portable nets and had to line the courts. It would take time to set it up and break down after."

"It was kind of a nightmare, but we did whatever it took to play and the whole club would help out."

"Obviously, now we all play with the proper courts. But it did make me appreciate it a little more after all that time of manually doing things."

"Now I go to other universities too and they've got like 16 courts," says Noah.

"It's really cool to see how much pickleball has grown just because most universities still don't have any courts."

"We were still just a club with me, a buddy, and another girl helping," says Noah.

"We structured it how we wanted to, ran the local tournaments very unofficially, and didn't get much funding at all. It was just kind of for fun and very grassroots. Nothing like varsity by any means."

"I started looking at the local tournaments with SDSU, UCSD, and USD and kind of realized that there's a need for organized college play."

"I started my preparation phase gathering contacts and calling over 250 universities in my dorm room while my friends were playing Halo in the other room."

"I needed a database, and for something to happen," says Noah.

"Once I got that first of 50 colleges, it just kind of sparked from there, and the word started to spread."

"When I started it was perfect because I would DM every college club I could find. That's how I got a lot of backing and contact. It helped tremendously."

"If I did that now, they would not respond because they get blasted by so many people."

"It's been pretty good," says Noah.

"I will say there's so many pickleball companies right now, whether that's apparel or random tournaments or apps that are popping up. A lot of people are starting to hyper-focus on reaching out to colleges and sponsor the clubs just to give them free apparel, shoes, whatever they can."

"I actually have an unpopular opinion about social media. We do live streams, and we try to put it on platforms like Instagram to make it look legit."

"This is kind of an NCAA-quality type of sport that we're building. I don't think social media is going to do much because people still haven't really bought in fully to the college side of things being the future."

"It starts with the players themselves spreading the word to other local universities," says Noah.

"It's going to be very grassroots because universities aren't going to invest into their club teams and then eventually varsity teams, unless there's enough to make it worth it."

"There's maybe two hundred that have a club, with 75% of them competing."

"Until we get to that four hundred mark, I think it's going to continue to be built grassroots."

"I've been asked if I'm looking to sell, or take on investors," says Noah.

"Only 24, I have a passion for the youth side of pickleball. I'm still young enough to connect to the college kids, but that won't last."

"Now is the time to establish the relationships and show why I chose to take this path in business. It has not been easy, but it's been worth it. Even if I have had to sacrifice material gains."

"God put pickleball in my lap. It could have been soccer, as I considered pursuing a professional career. But I just lost the flame for that."

"I knew I was called on to bring college kids together, to pray before events and to show them there is more to life. I show them how to be intentional, to love people, and pursue something meaningful."

"I'm a big believer in giving God the credit when it's nothing and when it becomes everything, right? However small or however big, I'm going to give God the credit," says Noah.

"From the moment I started this thing, I chose a Bible verse that I was going to make very public. It's on the homepage of our website" (Matthew 7:13–14).

"I make it very clear. Christ is at the center. I can't tell you how many conversations I've had with people approaching me saying not only 'we think this is so cool,' but also asking to talk," he says.

"And it just opens doors for people drawn to Christ. When you talk about Jesus in everything that you do, the conversations I've had have just been genuinely beautiful. It's just so cool."

"I had this twenty-year-old kid from SDSU come up to me and say, 'Hey, Noah, I'm starting to get serious with my faith. I just lost my dad. And it just kind of woke me up'."

"We kind of poured out our testimonies and our stories, right in the middle of the event."

"I love pickleball because of the elements of it bringing people together. I could have ended up in any kind of industry, but God put me here," says Noah.

"I'm not a rabid player. I love the game because of the community, because you can touch people and interact and open conversation. Maybe it's harder to get them to church. Maybe it's impossible to get them to church. But I can get them on a court. I don't care how the tribe comes together. I care that the tribe comes together. So that's how I see the game."

Paul Olson

A Man, A Van and a Plan

A high-level tennis player, Paul was introduced to pickleball by a friend.

"One of the guys in our tennis group passed on having coffee after a match because he was going to play pickleball."

"My friend Dave Werner was in great shape, and I thought, if he is doing this, I better find out what pickleball is, so I went and played."

"At the time, I had a very bad knee that only allowed me to play tennis about one day a week (it's been replaced since)."

"I found that I could play pickleball and rest a day. So, I started being able to go back to being able to play three days a week. And I loved it."

With only a few elite players in Minnesota in 2012, Paul had the opportunity to learn from the best.

"My friend Dave had played in some national championships. So, I got an opportunity from being a good skilled racket sports person through tennis to migrate into it fairly quickly."

"I got to learn the subtleties and the nuances of pickleball right away," says Paul.

"And that really piqued my interest because it was such a cool new athletic endeavor. As a doubles specialist in tennis most of my life, finding creative and interesting shots to make in pickleball was right in my wheelhouse. So, I converted instantly."

In 2013, the sport USAP proudly broadcast the fact that they had 150,000 pickleball players in the world.

"A few years later, there was an interview done in the Minneapolis Star Tribune about the future of 55-plus communities, and what the future held in store," says Paul.

"The executive from Dell Webb said they will never ever again build a 55-plus community without a major pickleball presence in it. This is the group that started in Sun City, Arizona, Sun City West, Sun City Grand. I think they're the biggest 55-plus community builder in the world. And they somehow got the vision."

As the weather began to cool, Paul's friends were heading south for the winter.

"I had to try and figure out how to surround myself with some other people who were pretty good athletes."

"I got very lucky, and I found a volleyball facility that was being built for a junior Olympic development club for girls' volleyball."

"I met the owners, and they said, 'Our club is wide open in the mornings. It's not used at all until the girls get out of school. If you want to play pickleball, go ahead and do it.'"

"In 2014, I started creating an indoor pickleball club," says Paul.

"My primary interest was growing and surrounding myself with other experienced ex jocks and jockettes. We developed a very cool recruiting process where there were eight or ten of us playing, and we would invite friends in to try the game."

"If we got eight to ten new athletes to try pickleball for the first time, four to five of them would join the group. Now we had twelve to thirteen good prospects. We repeated that every month in the beginning."

Paul's effort led to him setting up an academy to help teach others how to play.

"When I left Minnesota in 2018, I was running about 115 people a week through Champions Hall learning pickleball. Playing on a wooden basketball floor, the balls would skid like crazy," says Paul.

"But that's all we knew because we were in Minnesota and needed to be indoors for a long winter."

"I was divorced and was trying to figure out what I wanted to do with my next stage in life. I didn't know what I wanted to do," says Paul.

"My kids are grown, so I went to Mexico to try and develop pickleball there. I wasn't trying to build a business, just expand the sport into Latin America. I tried to develop a large pickleball center to host major events. But getting investors in my efforts was tricky in those years."

"I met a guy in Ajijic, Mexico named Joe Brook," says Paul.

"He had been the Davis Cup tennis coach for Singapore and spent his whole life coaching and running elite-level country clubs. Having just discovered pickleball, Joe wanted to give the game a try."

"It only took him a few weeks to become a solid 4.0 player, so we partnered up and qualified for the nationals one year."

Needing to import paddles for the new players in Mexico, Paul met Selkirk.

"They were this young up-and-coming company that worked very hard to help me to turn inventory. I was their first international customer."

"When I couldn't make things go in Mexico, I decided to go back to the States and play pickleball at the best places in the USA."

Paul had no plan of action.

"I thought, what's the worst thing that can happen? I'll lose 10 or 12k on this van the first year. I remember my daughter asking me, 'Are you gonna be parking your van down by the river, Dad?'"

"And I said, 'I will be down by the river if there are trout in the river!'"

"I decided to spend my entire summer driving all over the Western United States, playing in the pickleball places and fishing the best trout spots in North America," says Paul.

"I have now been in all 50 states in those three and a half years."

"My first summer turned into three years on the road, non-stop!"

"I bought an RV and traveled the country for three and a half years," says Paul.

"Selkirk asked me to become their national brand ambassador because of all these places that I went to and my background in the sporting goods industry. It was the perfect match."

"Part of my original arrangement with Selkirk was that they beautify my whole van rig," says Paul.

"I was even featured in an In-Pickleball magazine article that was called 'A Man, a Van and a Plan.' In the magazine article they did a full photo spread on me and my rig."

During a trip across New Mexico, Paul gets a phone call.

"It was Rob Barnes from Selkirk and he said, 'What are you doing in New Mexico? I just got a friend who passed you on the interstate!'"

"I wondered how Rob knew where I was traveling. It was that van that gave me authenticity in my travels."

The relationship with Selkirk continued to flourish.

"After the first, I went on a retainer, and after great success, they doubled it the next year," says Paul.

"In 2023, they approached me about doing a podcast for Selkirk TV. That was really game-changing for me because it gave me an authentic reason to be connecting with the movers and shakers in the sport."

Paul has now recorded nearly 100 episodes for his podcast, The Future of Pickleball, on the Selkirk TV app.

Each year, Paul would spend the first few months in Arizona.

"There's a legendary pickleball facility called the Surprise City Courts in Surprise, Arizona, which is where USA Pickleball was created."

"I played with two of the men that were the first two presidents of USA Pickleball. The pickleball was so good there, I ended up buying a house close by."

The Selkirk van got attention everywhere he went.

"I was dressed head to toe in Selkirk gear and was always looking for the 'Big Dogs' in pickleball when I got to town," says Paul.

"Everybody wanted to meet me and find out more about what I was doing. I played games, met so many friends, and always got invited for drinks after playing. My cell phone must have over 2,000 pickleball contacts in it now."

"USAP Ambassadors were always a big thing, and they were a real contact point for me," says Paul.

"Very often, I was going to places to play and had to search the web to find people. So, I stumbled across an old friend named Bob Kaiser. We hadn't spoken in nearly 25 years."

"Bob had become a pickleball ambassador in Ohio, and just set up a tournament in conjunction with the Arnold Sports Festival (Arnold Schwarzenegger). This was an amazing coincidence since Bob and I had met many years before in the ski industry."

"I'm on kind of a major passion project right now with all of the stuff that I've done and been involved within the sport of pickleball," says Paul.

"I think the next major moment in pickleball is establishing a true international governing body for the sport. The Global Pickleball Federation seems to be leading the charge and has a great group of talented people to make it happen."

"The minute pickleball becomes an Olympic sport is when the game of pickleball is legitimized globally."

In Dubai, UAE recently, Paul was the master of ceremonies for their first international pickleball conference.

"I'm always talking to people in other countries who want to bring in the game who know the United States is leading the charge with the sport."

"It's really been interesting to see the differences in other countries, and how our city parks operate differently than the rest of the world," says Paul.

"It's contributed massively to the success of pickleball, because the basketball and tennis courts are already there. Other countries around the world don't have the park systems we do."

"The leaders in foreign locations must be very creative. It's been fun to see all their ingenuity to make pickleball work in their countries."

Most countries in the world don't understand people over 50 still wanting to be athletes.

"There's nothing societally that fits them," says Paul.

"In pickleball you can be casual, you can be serious, you can be competitive. You can do whatever you want, and you can surround yourself with a whole bunch of fun, cool people no matter what your age. That's a unique module in sports."

"I want to be around people who are still choosing to be active. Maybe they kayak, bicycle, or hike," says Paul.

"Most of my older male friends from back in the day are old guys who sit on a couch back home. I don't have anything in common with them."

"As a single older adult, I can travel anywhere, play pickleball and have an instant community of new friends."

Paul loves being the "Road Warrior" of pickleball.

"I love pickleball because it allows me to be an athlete as an older person," says Paul.

"My pickleball game today is better than it was 13 years ago when I started playing. It changes because I'm no kid anymore. But the ability to have something that has a strategic advantage really fits my skill set."

"It's an amazing sport. I'm not sure if they designed it by mistake or actually the way that they did because every piece of it is built for socialization."

Rick Barry

All Star of Pickleball

A Basketball Hall of Famer and a four-time world long driving champion in golf, Rick was looking for something else to do.

"They got rid of our age category in long drive, and I couldn't compete anymore," says Rick.

"So I needed to find something else to keep myself active. My wife suggested pickleball. I had no idea what she was talking about. I decided to do some research and give it a try. I hated the kitchen when I started but quickly realized you couldn't have a game without it. I was hooked! My goal was to become good enough to win a national championship."

"I learned about The Villages, which was near my Lakewood Ranch, Florida, home. Pickleball is huge there, with over 300 courts," says Rick.

"They also have some excellent players, and a few in the Pickleball Hall of Fame."

Rick hooked up with an instructor there named Dick Scott.

"Dick introduced me to the game, and some great players who helped me speed up my learning curve over the next two years. I was also introduced to the founders of Engage Pickleball and used their outstanding paddles at the beginning of my career."

"Then a friend, Jeff Johnson, with whom I played a lot, asked me if I wanted to play in a tournament in Punta Gorda, FL," says Rick.

"Jeff was a solid 4.5 player, and he thought we could compete against the 50-year-olds. Both of us being ultra-competitive, we set our sights on winning. We did, and that was all the motivation I needed."

Rick was ready to compete nationally.

"The first event coming up was the US Open in Naples. But it was too late to register. Then, out of the blue, I got a call from someone in The Villages and was asked if I wanted to partner with a friend of theirs in the US Open."

"I entered the men's doubles 4.0, 70–74 age category," says Rick.

"Then I received another call. It was an invitation to play 4.0 mixed doubles. I said sure! So, by sheer luck, I got in not one but two events, and thanks to my partners, Greg Brents and Linda Bruder, we won gold medals."

That tournament was the start of a full schedule of playing.

"I was working with Don Shaffer, an owner of Medicileaf, a cannabinoid company that sponsored the PPA Tour," says Rick.

"That allowed me to play all over the country, where I won many gold medals with my outstanding partners. After a few years, I concentrated on the four majors: the US Open, the USA Pickleball Nationals, the Huntsman World Senior Games, and the U.S. Senior Pickleball Championships."

"Back then, Anna Leigh Waters and Ben Johns dominated the pros, winning multiple triple crowns," says Rick.

"So, I decided to try singles and see how my left knee, with no cartilage, would hold up. I thought, *how many hits can there be in a match between two old guys?*"

In 2024, Rick decided to try to win triple crowns in the four major tournaments.

"I won gold medals in all the singles very easily, and in men's doubles with my friend and longtime partner, Fred Shuey."

"Then in mixed doubles, I won gold in the US Open with Sue Matthews and gold medals at the Huntsman World Senior Games and the USA Pickleball Nationals with Alice Tym, who was a top pro tennis player back in the days of Billy Jean King. Unfortunately, we came up short and lost in the US Senior Pickleball Championships finals."

Rick won 11 of the 12 gold medals last year and almost had four triple crowns.

"Now I have a record that will be very difficult to match, but I was hoping to get a record that could never be broken."

"Because if I had gotten that last gold medal, nobody could have ever broken that record. The only thing they could have done would be to tie it."

"Pickleball has been great for me," says Rick.

"I love to compete, and it's been an absolute godsend for me to get out there and have a challenge. But I'm also a bit crazy because I like coordinating my clothes when I play. I want to look good on the court."

"Recently, I was sponsored by Selkirk, and played with their gear for a few years," he continues.

"I liked their paddles and did well, winning lots of gold medals. They are a great group. I attended charity events like Danny Wuerrfel's event and also the PGA Show."

When working with a company, Rick prefers to be involved in a meaningful way.

"So, last year, I joined Titan Pickleball and had great success with their outstanding paddles. I am excited that Ken Tran, the owner, wants me to do many more promotions and get more involved in the company's success. Reviews of their paddles have been impressive."

"I talk to many current and former pro basketball players about picking up the game. It's fun, and you always get a good workout," says Rick.

"I shared the game with Chris Mullin and saw Kevin Durant playing. They know how good the game can be for hand-eye coordination, and basketball players have all the necessary skills. Even Luka Dončić of the Lakers is playing pickleball this offseason. Pickleball gives you another sport where height, reach, and coordination are significant advantages."

"I love it when I'm up at the kitchen line and my opponents attack me by hitting a drive. My legs aren't what they used to be, but my hands are still pretty good. So, I love it when they challenge me."

Rick thinks the scoring in tournaments needs to change.

"It's not as important when you play for fun. But in tournaments, I believe rally scoring is the way to go. The scoring eliminates the amount of time waiting between matches. Now it sometimes takes forever."

"I had to wait an hour and a half between matches once in Atlanta. Waiting becomes an ordeal. And the older you get, the harder it is to play hard, sit, and go back out and play again. It's just ridiculous. Play needs to move along quicker."

"My wife, Lynn, is a 4.5 player, but will never play in tournaments. She was the only woman to have her basketball jersey retired at her alma mater, William and Mary, and is also a single-digit handicap player in golf. Years ago, we won the Colorado Springs mixed doubles championship in tennis."

Rick believes rally scoring will be the future of the game on TV.

"It allows more control of the games, and the time the match has on TV. With the current scoring system, you can't control when the games are going to be over. The TV side of pickleball is fun to watch."

"When I turn on my big screen TV, it goes right to the Pickleball Channel so I can see replays of past matches. Some of the points I see are truly amazing. You see very few unforced errors, and the shots they make are just off the charts. The angles they hit are amazing, and I love how players can now challenge line calls in some tournaments."

"We need to promote the players and the game more," says Rick.

"What Anna Leigh Waters has done in the sport is remarkable. I met her and her mother when they were playing together years ago, and the first thing I said to her mother was, 'I'm jealous, because you are playing professional pickleball with your daughter.'"

Rick believes that pickleball will never have another Anna Leigh.

"Never again will a 14-year-old girl come in and be the best pro pickleball player in the world."

"My son, Canyon, could be a 5.0 player if he ever decided to commit to the game. I am hoping for him to play in a tournament with me that I am attempting to have Chicken N Pickle host," says Rick.

Rick's idea would be to have a "combined age" tournament.

"We could compete well in the 110 plus years age and 4.5 skill bracket, because our combined ages work. Even going up against two good fifty-five-year-olds, we could hold our own. Playing together in a tournament with Canyon would be awesome."

Rick still plays recreationally, but open play is not much fun for him. He goes to the court for advanced players, and people who are 3.0 or maybe 3.5 players show up. You can't have a game when that happens. So, he works on hitting different types of shots to improve his game.

"My wife is so proud of me for being social, even though I tell her I don't do social well. I can do the social afterwards," says Rick.

"If I'm stepping on that court to play, I'm out there for one reason and one reason only: to win. It's difficult for me, but I'm getting better at it. And you do meet some nice people."

Rick has never seen a sport that has caught on like pickleball.

"It's not going away because it's easy to learn and pick up. Three years ago, I remember a big article saying there would be 30 million people playing in the US by 2030. We're in 2025, and over 45 million people are playing. So, I think that they underestimated them a little bit."

"The game has changed already in the years I've been playing. It was mostly dinking," says Rick.

"With the new power game, everybody has started hitting hard rocket shots, topspin forehands, and are attacking people. I love it when they attack me because my hands are excellent. Of course, now I hit the ball like a banger way too much."

"I want to get involved in more tournaments to raise money for charity, but the problem is trying to match up players because you don't have the handicap system like you do in golf," he says.

"It's difficult to get enough people in the right skill categories to have a meaningful competition."

A tireless ambassador for pickleball, Rick hopes that everyone gets to experience the sport.

"Anything you can do to get kids involved in something that can be a meaningful endeavor where they can have some fun, I'm all for it. I hope it gets to that point. That would be great, and I'll do whatever I can to help promote it."

"I just pray God will keep me healthy enough to play pickleball and go fly fishing till I'm 100 years old."

Riley Palmer
The Queen of Pickleball

Riley's first exposure to pickleball was with some friends. "We really had no idea what we were doing and just made up some rules. Sometimes, in between points, we would stop and do yoga."

"A few years later, I was going through a divorce and had to figure out how not to fall apart. So I decided to visit the local courts, meet some new friends, and try pickleball again," says Riley.

"One of the guys on the court was Danny Jensen, who's now a pro player. They all invited me to play, even knowing I was new to the game. They told me the rules, where to stand, and how to position myself. I was so nervous, and they were so nice to me."

Pickleball became Riley's safe space.

"I could just take my mind off of everything and enjoy my new community of friends. Nobody knew what was going on except me. I kind of traded in 'court time for court time'."

"I think it took a lot of stress off of the situation for me. And I think it drove my ex-husband crazy because he said I looked happier than I had been in a long time."

"My kids did a 'pickleball intervention' on Christmas Day, and made a funny, and somewhat realistic, video that went on TikTok," says Riley.

"By the fall of 2021, I was all in, and the game consumed my life. I was so excited about pickleball, and I wanted to kind of put forth like a real positive energy for myself too."

In one of Riley's first videos she posted playing pickleball, someone commented about her happy feet.

"It wasn't a compliment as I had to work on technique. So, I started to take lessons."

"The coach told me to stop playing with my friends and focus on more practice and instruction time. I was hooked."

"Once I started playing in tournaments, I sought some coaching mentors. One of them was Matt Panegasser out of Cabo," says Riley.

"He was so kind to have me come out and do a multi-day clinic. It helped my coaching take off."

Riley is on court more than twenty-five hours a week.

"I'm the director of an indoor pickleball facility, one of the head pros at the JW Marriott Desert Ridge here in Phoenix, and I rent a private court at a beautiful house nearby with all my equipment," says Riley.

"I love coaching couples, because those that play together, stay together," says Riley.

"I have a number of clients that I would have thought were in their second marriage. They act like newlyweds and treat each other with such kindness, respect, compliments, and concern for each other's safety. Some have been married for over 50 years."

"Three of the couples I teach met here while playing pickleball, and now they are married."

The majority of Riley's clients have some type of potency in their life.

"I see empty nesters, divorcees, and even some battling addiction," says Riley.

"Some of the younger guys I coach are sports betting addicts in full recovery who have lost everything in their life. So, we show them how to replace one addiction with another: pickleball."

"I love to see a player shut down initially, then open up as we get to know each other. It helps me know how to coach them and share the love for this amazing game."

"When I felt broken and got onto the court, the people I played with didn't know I was in the middle of a crisis. I learned and now I teach. It's become kind of a calling for me. I feel so lucky."

"It's been really fun having grown up out here in the Scottsdale area," says Riley.

"I've seen people and then they'll say, 'She's the queen of pickleball. That's who you need to go take lessons from.' It makes me feel good."

One of Riley's favorite stories is about someone she grew up with.

"His name is Ben, and we have been dating," says Riley.

"He wasn't into pickleball for a while but eventually asked me to give him a lesson. I was so nervous, and it was the worst lesson I ever gave. After that, he didn't want to go back to the courts for several months."

"But this weekend, he's playing his first tournament with my daughter. I'm so excited!"

"My newest adventure is in travel, as I recently launched Floating Pickle," says Riley.

"The last 25 years, my mom has been very successful doing international charter trips. And as my business is picking up, hers was too and asked for help."

So, Riley decided to do a pickleball trip to Croatia.

"I found pickleball players in Croatia on social media. I looked at websites."

"And so I made an online relationship with a lady out there who was kind of running the charge for pickleball. They were so excited we were coming out that they threw their first ever pickleball tournament in Makarska."

"It was so exciting," says Riley.

"They had some media there with players from England and Italy, and the tournament event made the cover of a local magazine."

"Over there, the players actually smoke between sets. But the Croatians are just wonderful people. They're so kind and they love Americans."

After that, Riley knew she wanted to do a cool charter trip in Croatia.

"I thought, okay, I want to charter my own yacht and then have a pickleball focused itinerary."

"What I found is that there are few places to play pickleball. We had to put a lot of work into locating courts at resorts and getting them set up."

"Halfway through the process, we came up with an idea to build an inflatable court to put on the side of our yacht," says Riley.

"We thought it would just be a cute photo op where we would take a few pictures. But our guests loved it and played for two days straight on the floating court."

"You get to play at the swim stops. That's the coolest thing about the yachts," says Riley.

"You stop in some private cove, and the water is breathtaking. And then you can jump off your yacht into the water."

Her team also decided to add a "skinny court" on the top deck of the ship.

"I play skinny singles with my dad and my nieces and nephews because you're not running around, but you're still working on placement and tactics."

"A big goal for me is to help pickleball grow more in Greece so that they have the coaching and facilities," says Riley.

"That's a big part of getting it in the Olympics. You can't just say you're going to host the games without the infrastructure. To me, pickleball is a universal game where people can all get in and play."

Sandy Halkett

Adaptive Pickleball

Ten years ago, Sandy's kids were getting ready to go to a theatre camp.

"One of their friend's dads came to pick them up and he was just drenched in sweat, and I asked if he had gone for a jog or something. He said, 'No, there's a gym two minutes from here and I play pickleball.'"

"I kind of laughed at the name, never hearing of it before. So, I asked him what pickleball was."

After being told about the game, Sandy was invited to come check it out.

"So, I did. The rest is history."

Back then, the pickleball scene in Greenville, SC was just getting started.

"There were probably forty of us playing at that time. We used to chalk the courts and use milk jugs to lower the net because there were no pickleball nets, or go ask a gym if we could put tape down."

Finally, Sandy got the facility to paint lines for pickleball on the tennis court.

"They did it wrong, as the lines were a foot short on each side. But we figured it out and played on them anyway."

"Soon after that, we went to speak at city hall meetings dressed in neon yellow," says Sandy.

"We were getting run off the tennis courts and making people upset. It was time to get courts for pickleball. The city and county listened, got us the courts, and the game has exploded since."

Now the area has a website called Upstate Pickleball.

"You can find places to play, events that are listed, and find a game just about anywhere."

"Our community has over 4,000 players and nearly 200 free courts to play on within a twenty-five-mile radius."

During the pandemic, people kept playing pickleball.

"Even though the courts were locked, we got creative and played in other places," says Sandy.

"We went back to the days of taping and chalking some community courts. Sometimes, I felt like we were sneaking around because we would play till we got caught. Even as grown adults, we acted like kids. It was fun."

"I can remember times when people would complain because we weren't social distancing, or too close to our playing partner, or sitting too close to someone waiting for a game," she continues.

"They even took pictures and turned us all in."

With everyone in isolation, there was a tsunami coming around pickleball.

"I'm sure if you look at pickleball net sales, I bet they went through the roof because people were playing in their cul-de-sac and their driveway."

"Remember people that had the nets and how popular they were?"

Sandy believes there needs to be a pickleball handicap system.

"We were playing women against men, and we decided to try it the last two games. I said, 'Why don't we play to 11, and you play to 15? That gives us a four-shot handicap.'"

"If we get to 11 or you get to 15, it's win by one. Like that's brilliant. The game was a lot more fun."

The daughter of a wheelchair veteran, Sandy became an adaptive golf instructor almost twenty-five years ago.

"I was teaching folks with cognitive and physical disabilities, and we also had a veteran community."

"A friend of mine came out to see what I was doing with golf and asked if I would consider doing the same with pickleball. He knew of my success winning lots of tournaments and my success in the community with adaptive golf," says Sandy.

"I had never thought of it and decided to explore the opportunity."

For two years, Sandy met with resistance at the hospital.

"I finally got to host a clinic right before COVID. They gave us some sport wheelchairs, and we had amputee and stroke patients come. All of them had some type of disability."

"So, with me knowing the sport and the therapist knowing their disability, we worked together just like we did with golf," says Sandy.

"I would ask if they can stand? How can they swing? Can they balance on the right side? Can they balance on their left side? And of course nobody wanted to leave the gym. They fell in love with it."

Inspired by others, Sandy created Adaptive Pickleball.

"We are dedicated to bringing the physical and social benefits of pickleball to people with diverse abilities throughout the Upstate South Carolina area."

"We see the smiles, hear the laughter, and feel the love every time we host a Pickleball Play Day. That's our motivation to grow the impact of Adaptive Pickleball. More smiles. More laughs. More love."

"Gary is an amputee veteran who was homebound with fear, anxiety, and depression. Socially, he just didn't know how to insert himself back into the world. He will tell you to this day that Adaptive Pickleball saved his life," says Sandy.

She saw the transformation before her eyes.

"Gary was a different person and felt like he had a reason to get out of the house and be active," says Sandy.

"He lost weight, gained friends, and always was excited coming to class."

Doing such remarkable things as a player, Sandy asked him to coach and get involved with the able-bodied students also.

"Gary has been amazing, doing whatever was asked. So, I asked him if he would like to be an ambassador."

"He was blown away and started crying. 'Y'all gave me my start,' said Gary. It's so great to see him embracing the game and helping others in their journey," says Sandy.

Adaptive Pickleball now has a global presence.

"I met a nice lady from Ukraine," says Sandy.

"She and I connected and talked every month for a year. And then she says, 'Sandy, I got to see what you're doing'."

"She got on an airplane and came over here and stayed a week with us to see what we do and how we do it. Now she's taken our model back with her to Ukraine to work with the military and the civilian population that has lost limbs."

"Growing always means we need more donations and volunteers."

"We are always looking to partner with companies in the industry. But we are careful to align, making sure that both sides truly have the same goals and purpose in mind."

"But if it's going to have APB on it, it's going to be 100%."

Sandy's kids laugh at her because she can't go anywhere without being recognized for her pickleball business.

"It might be at the grocery store, the restaurant, or just around town. Greenville is a big city, but we're not that big. Sometimes it's a connection from Clemson, sometimes it's a person I know from the golf industry."

"I guess what has surprised me is starting a nonprofit at fifty," says Sandy.

"We are still adapting the game, still figuring it out, and always coming up with new versions of pickleball to play with people with different abilities. Honestly, I never thought that Adaptive Pickleball would be part of my life."

Scott Moore

The Ageless Wonder

"About 13 years ago, I was becoming an empty nester and wasn't really happy about it," says Scott.

"I wondered, what am I gonna do with myself? Then God answered my prayer in a way I never would have dreamed."

A friend from playing volleyball together named John Foss knew that Scott loved racket sports.

"One day he asked me to try a game called pickleball, which sounded stupid to me."

"As soon as he told me it involved a paddle in my hand, I was all in. A racket sport junkie all my life, I had played five or six different racket paddle sports."

The first time playing, Scott was indifferent.

"We played probably once a month the first year. Half the time we had to shovel snow off the court, tape the lines, and put up our nets. So it was kind of a pain."

Scott soon got an invitation from his friend Ken Curry.

"He told me he was going to the 2013 Nationals, and his brother couldn't play, so would I be interested?"

"I said, Nationals? Are you kidding me? There's a Nationals in pickleball? Yeah, I'll go with you!"

Losing in the gold medal match to Hall of Famer Jim Hackenberg, Scott was hooked.

"That was it for me. I found my answer. I found my calling. I'm going to be the best player in the world in pickleball over 50."

Soon after, Scott jumped into his training.

"I had a karate friend and told him I needed to get in shape to become the best pickleball player in the world. He designed a little workout program for me, having never lifted a weight in my life," Scott said.

"I lost like 20 pounds and then got the biggest break of my pickleball career."

That April, Scott's son Daniel came back from a two-year work trip to Africa.

"He was a collegiate tennis player. I told him about pickleball and asked if he would train me so we could both become national champions. He was all in."

"We just had a temporary net and painted lines. Daniel and I were just going out to these tennis courts and playing three to four days a week. That was our training program."

"After hitting a lot of balls, we got really good and really quick in singles because that's what we played mostly and had played tennis all our lives."

When the father and son duo arrived at Nationals, they both easily won their singles divisions.

"Daniel won the 19+ and Open Pro singles and I won the 50+ and Senior Open Pro singles. Then we almost won the Open Pro doubles, losing 11-8 in the third game to the team that took gold. Honestly, neither of us really knew how to play doubles."

After becoming the number one pickleball player in the world in 2015 and 2016, Daniel told his dad he was moving back to Japan.

"I looked at him and said, let me understand this. You're going to walk away from pickleball being the number one player in the world and basically give that up to go back to Japan?"

"At the time, I was actually having more fun watching him win than I was winning myself. And we were winning everything at the time," says Scott.

"But it was his dream to go back to Japan, and he was fine with leaving the game at the top."

Arriving in Japan, Daniel started teaching pickleball.

"He was the first one to bring it to most of Asia, and has taught in seven or eight countries," says Scott.

"He's living his dream. It broke my heart when he walked away, but it's really worked out for him."

In addition to being a legendary pickleball player, Scott is also a serial entrepreneur.

"I've started over thirty businesses. The last seven or eight of them have been pickleball related. One of them is a pickleball facility called Espire Sports in Prescott, Arizona (espiresports.com). At the time we opened, we were the largest indoor facility anywhere."

"Our main business is called Pickleball Trips (pickleballtrips.com)," says Scott.

"We take people on pickleball trips around the world, while engaging the local culture instead of just hanging out at the resort. Over the last eight years, we have done over one hundred trips to twenty different countries."

"One third of our trips have been to Japan. That's where we raised our kids and my son Daniel lives."

"We're passionate about pickleball, travel, and adventure. Daniel and I have both been to about seventy countries individually. All my children, three boys and a girl, are involved in the company. It's truly become a family business."

"The pandemic effect was just absolutely phenomenal for pickleball. No one saw that coming," says Scott.

"We were also the first ones with an online academy. People were going crazy not being able to play pickleball. We literally sold a million dollars' worth of online videos through the pandemic and right after."

"Even though pickleball play slowed way down, we also had ownership in Paddletek, were instrumental in selling tens of thousands of paddles for them. The market just kept growing and growing. The business was growing so fast, we got carried with the rising tide."

"The last ten years have seen astronomical growth. It's unbelievable and a bit mind-boggling," says Scott.

"I had no idea it would grow this far and this fast. The technology, the athletic ability, and the international reach are just incredible. It has blown my mind. No question about it."

"One of our gifts to Japan is when we take our participants from North America over to Japan and play with the local Japanese players."

"They can't communicate, but they have so much joy and laughter and fun. We help them understand how to play, which the Japanese are not so good at because they value work so much. So that kind of reward is priceless for me, as we have grown to love Japan so much and wanted to be able to give back."

"It's also fun how many people we have reconnected with through pickleball, whether it be a high school friend or a college roommate," says Scott.

"There's a word in Japanese called 'deai' and it means basically 'encounter.' As one of my buddies put it, pickleball is the greatest thing he's ever seen at creating meaningful, social, competitive, joyful, sometimes even spiritual encounters. And that is really what it's been all about for me."

Scott said, "When I started winning a bunch of tournaments and became the number one senior pro in the world, my friend John Anderson pulled me aside and said, 'Scott, don't ever forget, it's all about the relationships.' At times, to my regret, I have forgotten and sometimes still do in the midst of the competition. But the best part of pickleball is that now we have friends all over the world and across all generations."

"I had no real connection points with the younger or older generations. No reason to have encounters."

Scott said, "And now I have encounters with numerous teenagers, twenty-somethings, that I get to play pickleball with regularly. That's one of the things I love about pickleball so much. It's so multi-generational and a lifetime sport. Meeting people of all different ages is so much fun. In my world, there are only two types of people: Those who haven't played pickleball, and those that will in the future. It's just a matter of time."

"My wife Susan will never say her last name when she goes somewhere, because she doesn't want to be associated with the assumption that she's a great pickleball player because she's married to me or is Daniel's mom."

"One of society's problems today is that social media is causing loneliness and isolation," says Scott.

"Pickleball gives people a reason to come together and have meaningful interaction and competition. I think for a lot of people's lives, mine included, it's just been nothing but a tremendous enhancement."

"I have one teenage friend who was completely addicted to social media and games. When he started to play pickleball, he lost 70 or 80 pounds and seems to have found purpose in his life," he said.

"The most meaningful pickleball experience I have had in my life was at 58 or 59."

"I had just won two gold medals in senior pro divisions at the U.S. Open," he says.

"On Saturday, I went to the stadium to watch the wheelchair guys play. They immediately called me out to play and told me to get in a wheelchair."

"I was really good when they hit it to me, but it wasn't great when I had to spin around and turn that wheelchair and go after the ball and whatever."

"After the game, we wheeled up and I had lost, and we touched paddles with the guys. And the guy across from me looks at me and goes, 'Hey, nice game, turtle.'"

"For the next ten minutes, I'm getting a lesson on how to maneuver the wheelchair and then step out and start walking off."

"And I was like, wow, they're so joyful. I'll never have a good reason or excuse for complaining again. That was so impactful, even more than my two gold medals."

"Recently, I got a text from a good buddy. Rick lives in Colorado and asked me to play in the wheelchair games in Colorado this summer."

"I'll be standing, and he'll be in the wheelchair, but if I can get in the wheelchair to play with him, I will."

"My favorite pickleball line of all time was about seven years ago in San Diego when I was just on top of the world," says Scott.

"It was raining, so we had to go indoors to play. My wife and her friend go to the intermediate side, and my buddy Bill and I go to the advanced side."

"She is greeted by the self-appointed pickleball policeman, who tells her that the courts are only for advanced players and that Scott Moore is here today

You can watch, but you can't play."

"My wife looks at him and says:Oh really? Because I actually slept with him last night."

He continues, "The guy was in shock, and started apologizing profusely. It was pretty funny."

"I've never seen people so excited to turn fifty because they can't compete with the younger players," says Scott.

"It gives people an ability to compete again. Even at sixty-three, pickleball has given me so much motivation to stay in shape and play professionally for as long as I live."

"Some days, I don't even realize that I'm exercising and staying in great shape because I'm just having so much fun playing three or four hours of pickleball."

Scott continues, "It keeps me younger, keeps me motivated, keeps me inspired. I am having more fun than I deserve at this age."

"I've been called a lot of things on the pickleball court," says Scott.

"But one of my favorites is the 'Ageless Wonder' because I'm the only person to have ever won a men's doubles (50+) and a master's men's doubles (60+) championship in the same APP tournament."

Scott also believes that pickleball is one of the only sports you can play your whole life.

"My stepdad played four or five days a week into his early nineties. I'm training to be just like him. If God gives me the opportunity to live that long, I'm going to do my part to be ready for the 90s."

Stephanie Lane

A Center Court Memory

Attending Lipscomb University in the late 80s, Stephanie was studying to be a physical education teacher.

"My professor wanted to teach us about pickleball. I thought she made up the word. Next thing I know, we are playing with wooden paddles. I loved it!"

"I didn't hear anything else about it after college until 2011," says Stephanie.

"A rec center nearby was having pickleball and I thought, is that the same sport that we learned back in college? Let me go check it out. And so, the rest is history. I laid the tennis racket down for good and have been playing pickleball ever since."

After waiting years for her hometown of Nashville to build some courts, Stephanie's patience ran out.

"I didn't think they would ever build pickleball courts, so my husband and I decided to put one in our backyard. It's now my happy place!"

Pickleball is everything to Stephanie.

"It's a life changing sport to me. I'm always sharing, always teaching, and always playing with beginners."

A board member with the IPTPA, she recently certified fourteen new instructors.

"It's an amazing sport that everybody needs to be exposed to."

In 2016, the US Open held its first tournament.

"Back then, we had to play at the East Naples Community Park and set up our own nets," says Stephanie.

"I have won several medals there, but my favorite moment was competing with Johan Svensson in 2018, when we upset two teams to get to the finals of the 50+ 5.0 mixed doubles."

"Two of our match wins were against Jennifer Dawson and her partner and Steve Dawson and his partner. We were not favored and surprised everyone," says Stephanie.

"Then Melissa McCurly informed us we would be playing on the championship court. I was trying to contain my nerves and enjoy playing in front of my biggest crowd ever. We made it a match, taking it to the final game before losing to Hall of Fame worthy competitor Brian Staub and recently inducted member Cammy McGregor."

Looking back, Stephanie has many fond memories.

"I had been there from the very beginning, teaching clinics right where center court is. And now I'm playing a match being covered by my friend Rusty Howes and Pickleball TV."

She continues, "Earlier that year, I was in the booth with him."

"It was the highlight of my career, and my favorite moment in a match."

"Pickleball provides great exercise, mental sharpness and a social connection for everyone," says Stephanie.

"I've seen people with disabilities or diseases like Parkinson's shaking before coming onto the court. But when we get a paddle in their hands and they're hitting a ball, it usually stops."

She is constantly amazed by how the game helps people.

"It gives them a new lease on life. I love how people can experience the thrill of a good shot and the camaraderie of the game."

She continues, "It really can change America because you don't worry about which disagreements or what people are on which side of the spectrum on different topics. We are all united. We are all equal. We're all humans who need to have fun and love. And it's just the most amazing sport ever."

Being so close in proximity on the pickleball court, you have to talk to people.

"If people are shy or they're not comfortable, you can eventually warm them up and have a conversation whether they're introverted or extroverted," says Stephanie.

"It just kind of forces you to interact when you're waiting for a game to play and you're next up."

"You really do kind of forget what life is and what problems you have."

Stephanie continues, "When you're out there escaping and just hitting the ball, and smiling and laughing and just socializing and competing, there is nothing better. Whether you win or lose, a bad day on the pickleball court is better than a day without pickleball, right?"

"My mom died unexpectedly when I was 14," says Stephanie.

"So, my dad took us to a resort for spring break, just to kind of get our minds off it. I met this guy from Canada; we became buddies and stayed in touch. Years later, he was in a parachuting accident and wasn't expected to live."

Her friend had some braces on his legs and was often confined to a wheelchair.

"So one time he traveled to the US and drove through my town. I invited him to play some pickleball in my driveway, and he fell in love with the game."

Stephanie continues, "Now he's playing wheelchair pickleball in the wheelchair event at US Open."

"It absolutely gave him a reason to live," she says.

"He went through a divorce too and had some personal issues with family at all. Pickleball literally gave him a new license to live and a new lease on life."

"I hope to be able to compete a little bit, even if it's not on the senior pro level anymore," says Stephanie.

"No matter the level of play, I still want to be competing and challenging myself. But most importantly, I want to be teaching the game to anybody who will listen so that they can have an experience of a life-changing sport like pickleball."

"Pickleball is a game that is so easy to learn, but so difficult to master," says Stephanie.

"I just don't think any of us will ever truly figure it out completely. There's just so many layers to this onion. Yet on the other side of the coin, you can teach somebody to play the game in five minutes. It's that funny sounding and quirky game that was created, and we all are so thankful that it was."

"I feel like I'm an ambassador to the game. Whether I'm at church, the gas station, or in my front yard, I feel like I'm always promoting pickleball. It's a life-changing activity. And once you try it, few people ever stop."

Stephanie knows you are never too old for the game.

"We can always help somebody else learn the game, even if we physically can't get around the court. I love certifying instructors and helping them learn how to teach the basics from the inside out, from the kitchen line back, no matter what age."

She continues, "I'll always be involved with pickleball somehow. It will definitely be a part of my life forever."

Tara Fieri

Passion for Pickleball

Wanting to hang out with her dad, Tara was invited to play pickleball with him and some friends at a local court.

"I really didn't know what to think about it and didn't know much about the game," says Tara.

"I ended up truly loving it, and seeing the competitive side of me come out. Having played college softball and other sports my whole life, I just missed competing in a sport."

Tara started playing pickleball in different places in Long Island and New York.

"When I started posting about it, none of my friends really understood because most of them were skeptical of the game and just didn't understand why I loved it so much."

"I feel like any kind of athlete with hand-eye coordination can play pickleball. Obviously there's levels and you have to drill and practice certain shots to become better at the sport. This makes it easy for athletes to cross over from other sports and play professionally," says Tara.

"What's so cool about pickleball is you don't age out and can play as easy or as hard of a level as you want."

Tara knows pickleball is more accessible and easier to learn than tennis.

"You can play with anybody with just a net on a court, and start dinking and practicing shots."

"I ended up signing a contract with Franklin Sports, which allowed me to be a full-time content creator," Tara continues.

"So I started my own events and marketing company, which allowed me to partner with like minded brands that I truly love and enjoy. It's evolved into a full-time career."

Playing in some pro-quality events at a 5.0 level normally, Tara loves to be able to compete, have fun, and get some wins.

"A lot of times in pickleball you beat yourself up after you miss certain shots, even though you are capable of hitting them. It's really just a mind game most of the time."

"I think the younger generation is the future of the sport because they're not transferring from tennis anymore. Their first sport is pickleball where they can compete for a scholarship in college. I wish that pickleball was my first sport."

"The social media community has definitely taken off and it's probably a little saturated," says Tara.

"There's a lot of people posting about it and there's no right way or wrong way to post about pickleball. That's why it's such a cool thing where everyone can have their own role adding some content, sharing creative concepts, and really just get people involved in every aspect of the sport."

Tara knows everyone has their own journey.

"I've always been a strong believer that people are unique. They may do the same things that you do, but everyone has their own unique way of making it special. There's no right way to do something. I mean, there's nobody that's played professional pickleball for decades and decades."

Every day, the sport grows. Says Tara,

"I love that in this sport, you don't have to be an Olympian or former pro to be a credible coach. If you know the fundamentals and can teach them well, you don't need to be the best player to be the best coach. There's value and credibility at every level."

"Pickleball is still so new. People are getting familiar with all the pro players and their personalities," says Tara.

"I think the industry is still trying to define itself, even in commentating the live game. So many still don't know what it feels like to see a game in person, and that needs to find a way to be shared."

Tara knows that as the pro player brands continue to grow and people relate more to them, it will drive the numbers of those watching the game up, allowing them to grow a bigger fan base on social media.

"It's exciting, as we are just getting started."

"Younger people definitely want to get more involved in pickleball," says Tara.

"You have some that are fully invested in pickleball and want to try it. And you still have those who don't think it's a real sport. Athletes and celebrities are now showing their involvement. This makes the sport seem cool and a little more relatable for the younger generation, especially if they already look up to one of them."

"When you see a big name like Mookie Betts picking up a paddle, it makes you think, 'If he's doing it, I want to try it too.' As more personalities outside the sport get involved, pickleball is only going to grow. The players today are reaping the rewards because of moments like this and because of the groundwork laid by those first wave of players who were out there competing when brands and TV hadn't even picked the sport up yet."

Tara has seen pickleball evolve so much.

"I mean, it's crazy. Almost all my friends are in the pickleball world. I even met my fiancé because of pickleball while working at the Super Bowl because I was hosting a Franklin Pickleball experience."

"We're definitely gonna have pickleball incorporated in our wedding for sure. The ceremony is at our family ranch, and we will build a custom court. It's going to be so much fun!"

"I always tell people to just go to the courts," says Tara.

"Don't be shy to just show up and ask people to hit around and play. You do have your pickleball snobs where they have their foursomes and that's it."

"But then there's the rest of the pickleball community that is always open to new players, and teaching others the game. And you have to start somewhere. Lots of players get intimidated by being on the court and beat badly. But you have to do that sometimes to get better."

Tara has always enjoyed playing at a higher level and getting beat.

"It always motivated me to want to compete even more. Plus, you never know who you will meet on the court. At the end of the day, everyone's there to play pickleball. It doesn't matter what background or who you are. Everyone can relate to one another because of the sport."

"I think people look at pickleball because it's like an escape from reality," says Tara.

"When I go on the court, it's like nothing else matters. A lot of times, my fiancé will end up texting me asking if I'm OK and when I'm coming home."

Like most, Tara loses track of time.

"After playing for two hours, you're just out there having a good time with your friends. You feel like a kid again just out there playing in the park until it's sundown. Your responsibilities just go away."

"In pickleball, you can play at a high level and compete with friends, or you can just look cute doing it and have fun. For me, I love to wear different outfits on the court and add fashion to the game."

Asked for her opinion of fashion and apparel in pickleball, Tara says,

"I'm the type of person who thinks if someone looks good in it, wear it. There's obviously brands that I love, right? And they may be more on the pricier side."

"But ultimately, if I go to Target and see something that I like, I'm wearing it."

"I think a person can make something look good by putting it together themselves. And I don't think that there needs to be a certain brand that you stick to and that's all you wear," says Tara.

"I love to put things from different places together to wear. I'm a firm believer that whatever someone feels the most confident in they should wear."

Boca Raton is becoming a center of pickleball. All of South Florida is building new facilities and courts everywhere. From 6 a.m., when you wake up and it's 80 degrees outside, there's people playing.

"My hope is to continue to really grow the sport, Major League Pickleball, and the National Women's Pickleball Foundation," says Tara.

"With everything I do, the focus is to be able to impact people's lives, put on quality events, and bring people together to network and have fun."

"I'm now a board member for the National Women's Pickleball Foundation," says Tara.

"Whether it's donating equipment, mentoring students, or bringing the game to inner city students, our Foundation has been created to support the game."

Working alongside organizations like Make-A-Wish Foundation and the Special Olympics, Tara loves seeing the smiles on the kids' faces.

"I would have never thought I could make a living in this sport, and more importantly make an impact. But when you put your passion and your purpose together, it's very powerful."

Timber Tucker
The Pickleball Jacket

"Just before COVID, I read about a charity pickleball tournament here in Bloomington," says Timber.

"Growing up a table tennis player, I thought this might be something I would enjoy. So I grabbed my young son to watch the event."

I decided to try pickleball the next day, and I showed up at the local park.

He continues, "I didn't know how to play. At least fifteen of the players were happy to get me started. I was addicted from day one."

Bloomington, Indiana, had few outdoor courts and no indoor courts, so Timber found an old warehouse and borrowed some roll-out courts to install.

"It's a win/win to have indoor courts for the team, the university club, and the community. One thing we quickly learned is we are not in the pickleball business, we're in the community building business."

Timber moved from head coach to the General Manager of the Indiana University pickleball club team. This allows him to concentrate on program building while more capable coaches focus on improving on-court performance. Timber sees the values of the game stand out.

"Even at the highest college competitive levels, college pickleball players are among the nicest people I've ever been around, and good sportsmanship really stands out. I love that."

"The men seem to have gravitated to the sport more quickly at the college level," says Timber.

"More want to play in college because they know they can be competitive and perhaps play at the highest levels."

He continues, "College women are harder to find at a high level. We look for women who excel at other sports. Tennis is obvious, but we've had success with former players of lacrosse, softball, volleyball, soccer, etc. They didn't grow up playing pickleball, but many adapt quickly with just a bit of coaching."

Last year's IU tryouts attracted 190 students. As of 2025, there are well over 200 colleges playing intercollegiate events. Many schools send multiple four-person, co-ed teams to tournaments.

"I've seen schools send as many as eight teams to tournaments. It just keeps growing, and growing, and growing."

"Here at Indiana, our club sport has a recreational division and a competitive division. The rec program puts together fun events for all students. They do campus tournaments, ladders, and other fun pickleball events."

Timber continues, "This year, we made a change to the competitive program. The 'Premiere' squad will be a more varsity-like experience. Many of our top players asked for something like this. I made sure they understood the commitment required, and they are excited about it. We will still have a 2nd competitive program for students who want to compete at a high level, but can't commit to the Premiere squad. We call this team our Challenger squad."

"I enjoy the heck out of watching our top players play," says Timber.

"We have national champions, college All-Americans, and a PPA pro on our roster. But it's often even more fun to watch a campus rec event. It's uplifting to watch a group of young adults gather for some fun."

"Last year I met an incoming IU freshman named Max," says Timber.

"Growing up, he had some health issues and spent a lot of time in a hospital. His dad and uncle attended IU, and he worshipped all the varsity teams growing up."

"Max is a solid player and made it through the first round, but he was eventually cut during try-outs," says Timber.

"After he didn't make the team, he still showed up at the facility almost every day. He came to drill by himself with a ball machine or to hit balls against a wall."

"When a spot opened up on the team, I picked him over a few of the more talented players. Max is exactly the kind of guy I want around the program. He works hard and is a team-first guy."

Timber continues, "We added him to the roster, and he was so proud to be called an Indiana Hoosier athlete."

Timber remembers, "At an evening practice, we were in our closing huddle and one of the team veterans asked Max to send the group off with our 'hands-in' cheer."

"Max cleared his throat, and in the deepest voice he could muster, shouted, 'Here we go, Hoosiers on three. One, two, three... HOOSIERS!' I had to turn away so the team didn't see me cry. It was just the coolest moment."

"I'm an Indiana University guy through and through. We are taught to hate all things Purdue," says Timber.

"But the IU and Purdue pickleball teams are weirdly close. It helps that both teams are just full of quality people. Each year, we have a competitive dual meet with the Boilermakers. Purdue hosted last year, and they added a pre-competition event that was a mixed doubles bracket, but each doubles team had one player from each school. It was a huge hit. My team said they had more fun with the mixed event than beating the Boilermakers for the 2nd year in a row ;)"

"This past year, we were at one of the national college tournaments. After the first night of play, I received a text from the Purdue team captain, inviting me to their Airbnb to play cards and watch the Purdue basketball game. I'm guessing this was the first time an IU 'coach' got an invite from the Boilermakers like that."

"The next few years may even be bigger than the last few for college pickleball," says Timber.

"I'm seeing younger children take it up as their primary sport."

"For the most part, the players on my team excelled in other sports as kids, especially tennis. That is already changing as we are seeing more very young players. DUPR has launched its first high school national tour."

"But I'm seeing lots of events in skilled divisions where 11- and 12-year-old children are crushing adults on the court. It can be a little humbling getting beaten by a 12-year-old, but I also make sure those kids know about IU pickleball!"

So what about the candy-striped jacket he's always wearing?

"That's become my signature look in college pickleball," says Timber.

"First of all, you can't buy that jacket. It was given to all of the men and women of the IU basketball team one year for Selection Sunday. It was a special release and was never offered for sale. A friend of mine on the coaching staff took a job at another school and gave it to me."

Tim knows his jacket is highly coveted.

"I've been offered $1,000 for that jacket. But again, it's become my signature. It's also so obnoxiously loud that my players can easily find me at college matches. Our team may be on 6–8 different courts at any given time, so it's an easy way for my players to find me when I'm flying around to different courts during matches."

"My personal pickleball crew is centered around my friend Ed. He's a beloved member of the community and owns a couple of popular local restaurants."

Timber continues, "He put a court in his backyard so his friends could come over and play. He added a pool, hot tub, and tiki bar," says Timber.

"He's happiest when his friends are enjoying themselves at his 'club.' Ed is always up for a good time. He's a busy dude between his businesses and family. So he put a Ring-style camera on the court, complete with a speaker and microphone, so that he can provide commentary on our play when he cannot join us."

"In the summer, many of the dads bring their kids to swim while we play pickleball. It has become a real-life 'Daddy Day Care.' I've never had a group of friends like this that I enjoy just being around on an almost daily basis to play bad pickleball and laugh."

A special story about Timber's pickleball group includes current tour pro, Mehvish Safdar.

"One day, Mehv showed up at the courts wanting to learn how to play pickleball," says Timber.

"Our entire group immediately adopted her. We thought we were teaching a novice, but we soon discovered she played Division One tennis in college. Within just a couple of years, she went from playing rec pickleball with her Bloomington 'uncles' to becoming the first college player ever drafted into Major League Pickleball."

When Mehvish was drafted by the Utah Black Diamonds, Timber immediately reached for his phone.

"I had to contact Connor Pardo, the owner of the team, because we all wanted to buy their gear and start wearing it now that she was on the team. She recently got traded, so we have to get some new gear."

Wilbur Matthews

Portside Pickle

"The first time I saw pickleball was in 1983 at Camp Longhorn," says Wilbur.

"The court was built out of asphalt, surrounded by chicken wire, and the paddles were cut with a jigsaw and glued broomsticks to the handles. I was the Camp Longhorn Pickleball champion that summer, and still have the activity award framed above my desk."

Fast forward to 2017.

"We were at a friend's ranch and there was a group of about sixteen of us from the country club."

Wilbur continues, "It was freezing cold that weekend, so we got hammered and played pickleball. We had the best time. My wife Catherine and I have played every week since then."

Back at the San Antonio Country Club, Wilbur would often walk by the men's grill with his pickleball buddies on the way to the courts to play pickleball.

"They would often comment as we were on our way to the courts, 'There goes the Pickle Mafia.' We even created our own group on WhatsApp with almost sixty people now," says Wilbur.

"The group turned into one of those management things and I was the commissioner," he continues.

"We would bring new people into the group and they would get in fights. And so then I would have to throw them out. It's the craziest thing ever."

"COVID is the thing that moved this game to where it is today," says Wilbur.

"And now, it's possibly the bridge that's going to save the community feel of this country because of a silly ass game with a plastic ball played on a small court."

Wilbur thinks of all the things that were done at his country club to get people to play pickleball during COVID.

"It was truly the first thing that reopened, right? Obviously you're not going to reopen the swimming pool."

He continues, "The country club reopened because there were a hundred people at the gates wanting to play pickleball. So they zip tied the gates open because we were going to tear down the gates if they didn't."

He calls this "pickleball pressure."

Now in Pensacola, Florida, Wilbur has teamed up to build his own pickleball facility.

"The short story is that we have a beautiful place of land on the water, and will have eighteen amazing courts both inside and out. To be honest, I'll always prefer the outdoors. But indoors gives you weatherproof certainty that you can play."

"It will be the most unique club in the country."

"I think that Portside is going to be a very important community place for people to just take a breath," says Wilbur.

"We want our club to feel like home where everyone can just lose time and be themselves. You can play one game, or stay all day long. So many people will take advantage of that."

"As we finish construction and prepare to open to the public, our main job with the club is simply not to mess it up."

He continues, "I think just understanding what the IT of pickleball is, is a big part of that. It's the intersection of social interaction, the elevation of the everyday player, and facilitating the 'just get me on the court/let me play vibe.' If we can figure out how to enhance it and make it better, that's good too. It's almost like one of those examples where if you just throw the ball and some paddles out there, good things will happen."

"What's funny to me is the number of people that say they're waiting for Portside Pickle to open," says Wilbur.

"Maybe that speaks to having done a good job of building a community. Our goal is to build a 'pay it forward' model, where experienced members will take a few minutes and welcome new players onto the court, and into the game."

At one training session with fourteen coaches, Wilbur was surprised to see some random people show.

"Our courts are not easy to see, but they found us anyway."

He continues, "As we are practicing, I look over and see four people standing on the side of the courts with paddles. I thought one of the coaches invited them but no one did. They saw us playing and wanted to join in."

"There is such a need for pickleball courts here that people are always peering through our fence wondering when we will open," says Wilbur.

"There must be some Facebook group dedicated to crashing the gates at Portside Pickle."

Another time, Wilbur noticed a couple peering through the gate.

"They asked about our progress, as they were moving from Birmingham, Alabama and wanted to know where to play pickleball because it was such a big part of their life back home."

He continues, "I found that very exciting because those are the kind of people that we are trying to capture and help build exactly what they had in another community."

"We are always fielding calls from people that want to do something here," says Wilbur.

"Even though we are not open yet, it's so hard to say no. One of the groups wanted to host a charity event around Halloween. I expected to have a few courts ready by then and said yes."

As the date drew closer, Wilbur realized they wouldn't be open in time.

"After getting agreement from the group, we decided to stencil out three courts in the parking lot, which wasn't in the best shape."

He continues, "We had a great time with about sixty kids showing up to play. It was a classic example of how pickleball can be played anywhere. It's hard not to have a good time in almost any pickleball environment."

Even before officially opening, Portside Pickle has an impressive following.

"We have 1,400 people on our email distribution list. The growth is just insane. Everybody's heard of it at this point," says Wilbur.

"We're still at such an early phase in the growth, evolution and adoption of pickleball that we get to write the rules. And that's the most exciting part of all of it, in my opinion."

"There's no rule book that we really have to follow. And there's so much potential with the blank canvas at our facility right now."

Wilbur continues, "A lot of our decisions have a purpose, but you can still get creative with others. It's not like other models where you have to follow a guide."

Portside Pickle is still being built.

"We didn't have pretty courts up until a few weeks ago," says Wilbur.

"But people still wanna know the before, during and after, and they wanna be brought along into the process, even if things don't look pretty, because that's the fun part."

He continues, "So social media wise, I'd say people like to follow along with a story and they want to be involved in that story. They truly value the information being shared."

"Females dominate the social media space big time. There's a lot of creators out there that are bringing you along in the journey," says Wilbur.

"And I think that's something that people have connected with. They want to learn how you go about your daily life in the pickleball space, and find out what it looks like."

He continues, "Some influencers document their day from the moment they wake up."

Wilbur thinks pickleball is less interesting to social media audiences than most think.

"Most true influencers in sports, media and entertainment have millions of followers. But our top players can't crack a few hundred thousand in total," he says.

"With some effort and a little investment, I bet I could beat our top pickleball influencer numbers in less than a year. I think the pickleball movement may very well be about rejecting mass media and embracing our humanity through face-to-face interaction."

"I think one of the most interesting stories I've ever read had to do with how long it takes to make a friend," says Wilbur.

"In order to make a friend, you have to spend about 200 hours together. What better way to do it, then on a pickleball court?!"

Wilbur knows the possibilities for this sport are endless.

"There are just as many opportunities for both females and males. The sport doesn't restrict achievement because it's always been run by the 'good 'ol boys club or anything else."

He continues, "Plus, there are things about pickleball that still haven't been invented. It's always evolving."

"I can't put my finger on what it is about pickleball that makes it so easy to get four people to go play, have such a great time and get addicted to the sport. But it's fascinating to me, and I'd love to figure it out. I feel like it's a riddle that I'm going to get the answer to. Someday."

Acknowledgements

Alyssa Morrison, Ben Shapiro, Billy McGahee, Casey Brown, Danny Jensen, Darren Lancaster, Ernie Medina, Genine Fallon, Jack Glasure, Kaitlin Miller, Kamryn Blackwood, Mark Zinno, Mick Tingstrom, Mike Sliwa, Noah Suemnick, Richard Walsh, Rick Barry, Riley Palmer, Rocky Clark, Stewart Davis, Tim Klitch, Timber Tucker, Wilbur Matthews

About the Author

Born and raised in Maine, I couldn't wait to get to Florida and start my college experience at Florida Southern in Lakeland. Since then I have lived equally in both states, partly by choice, partly by design, partly by personal obligation.

Divorced since '06, I have been blessed to raise a daughter. We formed a special bond on the softball field, and I remained her coach till the end of high school. When Alexandra graduated, it was time for my nomadic life to begin. I haven't looked back.

Many still ask me why I started writing. Truth be told, I have no idea. But with the release of *The Pickleball Effect*, I have found out how much I enjoy storytelling. What lies ahead is anyone's guess.

Fun Facts:

.Attended over twenty five Jimmy Buffett concerts

.Favorite Movie is My Cousin Vinny

.I have spent almost two years(in total) traveling throughout Costa Rica. "Pura Vida"!

.Received a black belt in the martial art of Tae Kwon Do

.Still a decent Bachata and Salsa dancer

I look forward to meeting many of you on the court, sharing a laugh, enjoying a game, and telling some stories!

www.ingramcontent.com/pod-product-compliance
Lightning Source LLC
Chambersburg PA
CBHW050103170426
43198CB00014B/2440